Maria Mitchell,
First Lady of American Astronomy

Maria Mitchell, First Lady of American Astronomy

Helen L. Morgan

W

The Westminster Press
Philadelphia

First edition

PUBLISHED BY THE WESTMINSTER PRESS®
PHILADELPHIA, PENNSYLVANIA

Printed in the United States of America
9 8 7 6 5 4 3 2 1

Library of Congress Cataloging in Publication Data

Morgan, Helen L
  Maria Mitchell, first lady of American astronomy.

  Bibliography: p.
  Includes index.
  SUMMARY: A biography of a feminist who was the first woman science professor at Vassar College and the first American woman astronomer.
    1. Mitchell, Maria, 1818–1889—Juvenile literature.
  2. Astronomers—United States—Biography—Juvenile literature. [1. Mitchell, Maria, 1818–1889. 2. Astronomers.
  3. Feminists] I. Title.
  QB36.M7M67   520'.92'4 [B] [92]   77–5871
  ISBN 0-664-32614-5

To my sister and teacher,
Gladys L. Powers,
and her husband,
Dr. Justin L. Powers,
of the University of Michigan

Contents

1

The Walk on the Roof

Outside the shop, someone called, "The *Ann*'s hoving in! She's off the bar."

Maria and her brother Andrew climbed up to the roof walk. Their father's cooper shop had once been a house, and like most houses on Nantucket, it had a railed deck on the roof, where a captain's family could watch the coming and going of ships. The lookout was rightly named widow's walk, for members of the ships' crews were often lost at sea.

All the life of Nantucket revolved around the whaling ships. Manning them or furnishing the crew with food was the island's chief industry in that year of 1831. Maria's father had a little farm that provided his family with vegetables, but the cooper business and his brother's whaling ships were part of the town's main industry. The casks had to be filled with whale oil for home lamps and for markets as far away as England, as well.

Maria was almost thirteen now and was used to seeing customers from many crews, swarthy Portuguese sailors with rings in their ears, tall fishermen from her own Quaker meeting, black men occasionally, and Indians from farther north. All of them bought the casks made by Mr. Mitchell's workmen. They used them as containers for salt pork at the general grocery store and for storing the crackerlike bread called hardtack, which, with occasional fish chowder, was the backbone of their diet.

Now the *Ann* was outlined against the sunset. Andrew said excitedly, "It's Uncle Isaac's ship, all right." His face lighted up. "He told me I could go with him, next voyage."

"I wish I could go!" Maria said wistfully.

"You can't. You're only a girl. You don't know much." Andrew's voice was scornful as he pulled his cap over his ears to shut out the cold wind.

"I know the ships sail according to the stars," Maria replied. Their father was a fine amateur astronomer, and she had learned the names of the stars and planets from going up with him to the little platform on their roof. He told her that she had seeking eyes and great curiosity.

"I could go if I tied back my curls and looked like a boy," she went on. "Anyway, sea captains' wives go on voyages."

"Who wants anyone on a tippy deck wearing skirts?"

"I don't wear skirts always. I usually wear your old pants up here when it's this cold."

"They were too tight for me. I outgrew them. You're only twelve."

Her dark eyes flashed, although that was a fact she could not disprove. But she knew she was sturdy even though she was small for her age.

That night as Maria helped her older sister, Sally, with the dishes, she remembered her brother's spiteful words. She wondered if Andy was really going to sea. He had seemed strangely quiet at supper and had gone to his bedroom early. He might be packing his clothes.

"Sally, better mind the baby. Maria's dreaming." The voice was stern. Their mother sat in the high-backed rocker, stitching on a calico square for a quilt. A white cambric bonnet and lawn kerchief shadowed her face. Her long nose made her seem severe. Maria believed that her mother could read minds. Perhaps, she thought, Mother knows I want to go on the ship, but then, she may have heard that Uncle Isaac wants Andy to go.

That night when Maria heard her brother slam his chest shut and bang a bureau drawer, she was sure that he was packing to go on the ship. Quietly she pulled on his old pants and an old coat and cap. After she tucked in her curls, she could see in her mirror that she looked like a boy.

Then she heard him pussyfooting down the stairs. Tying her shoes together and hanging them around her neck, she followed him, carefully avoiding the squeaky lower step.

As soon as Andy closed the heavy door, Maria rushed forward and crept outside, carefully latching the gate and following in the shadows. As she looked back, she thought she saw a dim light in the kitchen.

Andy was carrying a little chest, and he had a ditty bag slung over his shoulder. He began to run. Was he afraid he would get there too late?

It was more than a mile to the wharf. Morning was breaking by the time they reached there, but her brother had disappeared from sight. Maybe he was hiding. A swarthy sailor ran toward Maria holding out a paisley shawl. "Little lad," he wheedled, "it's my last chance to sell. The *Ann*'s leavin' early."

Hurrying on, she saw Andy walking toward a dory rowed by a sailor. When the man pulled up close enough, Andy jumped in and turned his back. With angry tears in her eyes, Maria turned away. Andy had never told her that he was to meet Uncle Isaac's man from the ship.

She shook her fist and almost hit the man with the shawl. As he turned away, muttering, "Took that boy

[11]

instead of me!" Maria realized that she was acting like a child, while this poor man had lost his chance on the ship's crew.

Now her eyes saw the dory as a blur against the sea and sky. Sometime I'll do something as wonderful as going to sea, she thought. I'll learn something about ships.

Soberly Maria retraced her steps. She remembered that she had promised her father to help him record an eclipse of the sun, of which he had received news from Harvard College. At the moment, he was away, doing a coastal survey for the Massachusetts government.

Andy had helped their father in the past, but he was more interested in ships and harpooning whales than in astronomy. He had seen sailors returning from whaling voyages with money in their pockets. Uncle Isaac had become a successful captain. If the ship returned with many barrels of whale or sperm oil, Andy knew he too would get a good lay, or share of the money, when the cargo was sold. Girls could never earn money that way, Maria thought ruefully.

On her way past the square log jail, she heard some drunken sailor singing "Blow the Man Down." He will stay there until he gets sobered up, she thought.

When she reached the gray-shingled house with its bright flowers poking through the fence, she looked up at the railed walk on the roof. She would watch there, someday, waiting for the return of Andy.

Suppose he didn't come back?

Tears came into Maria's eyes as she fumbled with the mahogany latch on the white front door. It, she knew, was a relic from the wreck of an English ship off Nantucket in the War of 1812. She didn't want to be reminded of shipwrecks.

Inside, she hurried through the little entry. Hating the thought of meeting her mother with the bad news, she

[12]

stopped by the parlor door. Her father had told Sally to dust the chronometer and put it in the parlor, ready for the eclipse. Maria opened the door and saw the ladder-backed chairs waiting stiffly, but there was no ship's clock. She had never liked the parlor, but her father had said the light would be better there for viewing the sky and they would be more comfortable than outside, where it was cold. Behind her, the grandfather clock struck then, and Maria turned to look at the friendly face inlaid with a golden sun, moon, and silver stars. The grandfather was always a reassuring presence in the gray room. However, they couldn't see the seconds on the big clock as well as on the chronometer, so she must bring the instrument in for the eclipse.

Hearing Sally talking to her mother in the kitchen, Maria slid into the sitting room quietly, glad to put off the bad news a little longer. Quickly she dusted the chronometer with a cloth from the bureau and put it on the parlor table, being careful not to joggle it and disturb its accuracy. There was a lever inside it to ensure even pressure of the mainspring. Now that the chronometer was in place, Maria thought the parlor looked more friendly.

The sitting room was Maria's favorite room. As a child she had loved the glass ball that was suspended by a cord from the center of the ceiling. It flashed rainbows around the room on sunny days. Her father used it for light experiments. In a cabinet near his desk were bright red and blue mineral specimens. She liked the pink roses on the walls and the bright carpet her father had chosen. The fireplace was cozy, with its piles of driftwood in bins on either side. From above the mantel, Elizabeth Fry, the great Quaker famous for prison reform in England, looked down with gentle eyes. Would she have known how to explain about Andrew's running away?

Maria opened the door of the kitchen and saw that her

[13]

mother was alone. Sally had gone into the woodshed. Mrs. Mitchell was kneading dough. It was early for her to be getting dinner.

"Mother, Andrew's gone off on Uncle's ship!" Maria said.

Mrs. Mitchell turned around and let the roll of dough fall to the board. "Thee's sure?" Her voice rose.

"I saw him leaving in a dory with a sailor."

Her mother stood silent for a moment. "He told me good-by, but I hoped he'd change his mind."

"He was set about going," Maria said.

"Then what's done is done," Mrs. Mitchell said and began to knead the roll of dough with quick, sharp thrusts. "Uncle Isaac will be a good ship's master, but Andy's young."

"But he's older than Sally and me. . . . I wanted to go," Maria blurted out.

"Girls can't." Sally had entered the room and was removing the chairs from the places parallel to the wall, the way Maria always arranged them. Angrily Maria straightened them.

Sally tossed her head. She knew that she was pretty, like the woman on a ship's figurehead, and that was important. "Thee's stubborn as a pig," she said. "Thee'll be an old maid, for nobody likes stubborn women."

Maria did not answer. The chair incident had been repeated many times. "We must hurry about smoking the pieces of glass so we won't hurt our eyes when we look at the eclipse. Father might get home early." He had told her to blacken some extra pieces of glass for the younger children to use when they looked at the sky.

About eleven thirty, William Mitchell returned. His face was less severe than Mrs. Mitchell's and there was often a twinkle in his eye. But today there were unaccustomed lines in his forehead as he said to his wife, "Thee

[14]

must have heard about Andrew, Lydia."

She nodded, as if she could not speak of their loss. Then she said, "Isaac Brayton keeps First day on his ships. He'll see that Andrew isn't in bad company." She sighed. "This bread should be done for the noon meal." She put the shaped loaves in the wall oven.

Mr. Mitchell bit his lip. Life had to go on as usual, even if Andrew was gone. "Sally will see the eclipse and then mind the twins," he suggested. "Maria and Ann will bring the younger children inside. Everyone must see the eclipse."

"Come, Ann," said Maria to her nine-year-old sister. "Tell William Forster to come in with Francis. I'll get Phebe. She's busy upstairs with her dollhouse. All the children must wear their heavy coats, because the window will be open and the parlor will be like Iceland."

"Thee mustn't keep thy father waiting," Mrs. Mitchell admonished.

As Mr. Mitchell carried the little telescope into the parlor, his wife brought the pieces of smoked glass. Maria heard them talking about Andy as she hurried to the stairway to call Phebe. Although the little girl was only six, she was good at minding the twins.

When all the middle Mitchells were rounded up, they filed into the parlor looking as if they were going coasting.

"Thee's done well with the glass," Mr. Mitchell said to Maria. "Bring thy notebook." Maria hurried to get it from her father's desk.

He took out the upper part of the window, and the bitter wind from the ocean cut through them. "Boo, I feel like an icicle." Francis pinched Phebe. She slapped him, and Maria pulled her away.

"We must have quiet so that Maria can count," Mr. Mitchell said. "When Maria stops counting, it will be the

[15]

beginning of the eclipse. Mother has the first glimpse, then Sally, then Maria. Then you're to come according to ages: Ann, William Forster, Francis, and Phebe. Henry and Eliza, we hope, will stay asleep and not yell. The eclipse will last three hours, so every member of the crew will have a chance to. look through the telescope after I raise my hand for the beginning."

The silence was broken only by the ticking of the chronometer and the low voice of Maria counting, "One, two, three, four. . . ." She bent over the chronometer, and the steady count went on until it was fifty-five minutes after eleven o'clock. Then she counted seven seconds. Her father raised his hand to mark the beginning of the eclipse.

He was checking with the time predicted by an astronomer at Harvard. It was important for scientists to know the exact second the first piece of the moon showed against the sun, for that was the way they found out about the moon's movements.

Maria wrote, "Eclipse, February 19, 1831," in her notebook.

"It will happen again in fifty-four years," Mr. Mitchell predicted.

"Then I'll be an old lady." Maria laughed. "I'm twelve and a half now and I'll be sixty-six and a half when the eclipse comes again."

A blob of darkness began to cover the sun. It was beginning to darken outside. The chickens ran toward the hen houses as if it were their bedtime. The screaming gulls were suddenly silent.

Each child took his turn at the telescope. As at last the black circle moved away from the sun, the dim light brightened. A rooster crowed far away, and then another one, and finally one in their own yard. To them it looked like morning. Maria would never forget that eclipse. At

[16]

that time she suddenly realized how orderly the universe was. God has a plan, she thought.

That night Maria went up to the widow's walk on the roof of the house. Her father brought his telescope, which was just a long tube with a lens that could be moved. He adjusted the telescope so she could look at the stars, facing north. "That's the Big Dipper," her father said. "See those two stars? They are called pointers. You could draw a line through them to Polaris, the Pole Star or North Star. It is at the end of the smaller bear's tail—Ursa Minor, we call it in Latin. You'll study Latin someday."

Hearing about the stars and walking on the beach, moorland, and marshes interested Maria more than school. She was glad to know about Polaris, but she doubted that she would ever lose her way and need help from the friendly stars.

Sometime later, on one of Maria's long walks over the moors, she saw that clouds were piling up in the northeast. It looks like a squall, she thought. Fog was forming like a thin curtain, but as she walked into a hollow, the mist became so heavy that she could not see the path. Her own home was on Vestal Street, but that ran into the main road and this road did not. She must now be on the way to the old settlement of Madaket.

The steady, majestic beat of the ocean reminded her of her favorite hymn:

> The spacious firmament on high
> With all the blue ethereal sky
> And spangled heavens, a shining frame
> Their great original proclaim.

But she couldn't see the heavens or the stars. The fog pressed against her with long fingers. She trudged onward until the curtain began to lift and she could see the

[17]

glow of a dim yellow light. There was a shack with a low door. It could be some fisherman's home, she thought, but it seemed far from the ocean. At least she would have a roof over her head. When Maria pulled on the latch-string, the door opened.

The only light was a candle flame. Her shoes touched something soft. Was it a pile of rags to keep out the cold or something alive? A cat streaked toward a dark corner. Maria laughed to herself. After all, she loved their cats at home.

"What's thee doing here?" A dark figure rose and lurched toward Maria. At least she's a Friend, for she says "thee," the girl thought.

The crone's face was smoked by the soot from the smoldering charcoal fire. Now that she was nearer, Maria saw that the woman's clothes were greasy. As her eyes became used to the half darkness, Maria could make out two more women on a settle nearer the fireplace wall. She recognized them as the Newbegin sisters, who came to Friends' Meeting on First day. Maria had heard that they were simpleminded women, needy but unwilling to be helped. I must have walked all the way to Madaket, she decided.

"Why did thee come?" the tallest one asked.

"I'm lost," Maria answered.

Looking more closely, the old woman said, "Thee's William Mitchell's gal. Thee's cold and needs something hot." Slowly she made her way to the kettle on the hob. Maria supposed that she must be Anna, the smartest one. Her hostess ladled some liquid that smelled like chicken broth into a wooden bowl. Then, as she pointed toward the disheveled bed, Maria sat down gingerly. Something seemed to be moving under the mattress. Sometimes poor people put hot potatoes under the quilts to make the

[18]

bed warmer. A little doubtfully Maria thanked Anna for the soup and sipped it slowly. The blind sister, Mary, did nothing but clasp and unclasp her hands. Phebe went on sewing, her head bent. At last Anna said, "Thee must stay the night. A body'd get lost forever in that fog."

Maria felt as if hands were clutching her. She must get away! She ran to the door and pushed it open. The fog had lifted a little. "I've got to get home. My father will be hunting for me. Thank thee for thy soup."

But when she started to walk, she stumbled. There was a wall of fog. The whole area must be in a hollow, she thought. She wasn't quite sure of her route, for the waves had quieted down and she couldn't be certain whether or not she was going toward the harbor. Trudging doggedly, she reached higher ground. Gradually the fog lifted. The moon peeped through. Then the stars. She must find Polaris.

There was the Big Dipper, and there indeed was the North Star, just as her father had shown her. Now, if she turned, she would be on the road to Nantucket and the gray-shingled home on Vestal Street.

As she opened the door of the sitting room, Maria found her father seated at his desk, his back turned as though he was busy. "Oh, Father, I've been lost!"

She ran to him, and he put his arms around her and held her close. "Calm thyself and tell Father." His kind blue eyes were reassuring.

"The North Star helped me find the way home. I want to study the stars."

"Thee must learn arithmetic, then, and higher mathematics after that. It's a long road, but we'll start today with the chronometer."

She looked at a box-enclosed clock on his desk. It was hung inside a framework of rings.

"Why does it have rings?" she asked.

"The chronometer needs these gimbels to keep steady when the ship rolls," her father explained. "We'll try to find out whether it is slow or fast tonight if it keeps clear so that we can see the stars. We'll need the sextant."

Sally burst in from the kitchen. "Thee can't see anything if the lampwick's dirty," she said. "That's thy task, Maria."

Being two years older than Maria, Sally always felt she must put in her two cents' worth.

"Of course. I'll do it now," Maria answered. "But tell me, Father, when thee wants me later."

Nodding, Mr. Mitchell turned to his notations. She knew that he had brought back records of the channels along the coast. He was humming as he transferred the data from his notebook.

In the kitchen, Maria scrubbed the whale oil lamp and put in a new wick. "Mind the twins," her mother said from the bedroom. "Now the fog's lifted, Sally can take the other children to the store."

Maria heard them leaving. Phebe and Ann went quietly, but William and Frank were yelling as they ran outside. When Henry cried, she changed his diapers and darkened the bedroom. Then she went to Eliza and rocked the cradle until she, too, was quiet.

That night Maria and her father got ready to go up on the roof. They took a whale oil lamp, the sextant, and the chronometer. The sextant was an instrument shaped like a piece of pie standing on its curved side. It had a small telescope and tiny mirrors.

Mr. Mitchell used the sextant to measure the altitude of the North Star and recorded the corresponding chronometer time. Then he repeated the observation on the star Gamma Cassiopeia, finding out by complicated mathematical procedures that the chronometer was two minutes slow. He set the chronometer by inserting a key as one would adjust a slow clock.

"I must study a lot before I can do that," Maria said. Her forehead wrinkled.

2

"I Want to Learn"

Sometime in the foggy early morning, Maria heard the town crier calling out the arrival of a ship. "Four o'clock and the *Baltic*'s in. Heard tell of the wreck of a schooner ashore on the north coast of Portugal."

Captain Bill Chadwick came to the Mitchells' later with more news of the shipwreck. The master of the vessel must have had a chronometer that was too fast, so he had reckoned the ship's position wrong and hit the rocks. Would the wives of the crew still watch from their widow's walks for a ship that never returned? Maria decided that she must learn more about the stars.

That night she saw her father working at the desk. "Could I ask thee some questions?" she asked quietly so that Sally could not hear. "I'm still puzzling over the wreck of that schooner off the coast of Portugal." She sat down in the chair where sea captains sat when they called on her father.

"If he had a chronometer, it might have been fast or slow, but not correct with the time in Greenwich, England. Of course thee knows we get time from the Royal Observatory in Greenwich by sailing ship chronometers, but that changes as soon as the ship leaves port."

"I wish there were some way to send messages faster," Maria said.

"Possibly the master of that schooner had no chronometer and therefore sailed it by compass. That's called dead reckoning, as thee knows from our own sailing. Probably he was carried onto the rocks because he was off his course."

"That's why we have to keep track of ocean currents along our coast," commented Maria.

"Thee wants to know more about using the stars to get the ship's position. In rainy weather we can't see the stars, so we can't use the lunar method as we did before. If the moon is bright, we can measure the nearest star's position from both ends of a base line, and from the difference in angle of the two star sightings the distance of an object can be calculated by plane geometry and advanced mathematics or trigonometry."

"It sounds hard," said Maria dubiously.

"Not when I help thee," her father assured her.

"I do want so much to learn," said Maria.

Maria's schooling had begun when she was four years old. She first attended dame school, a private school for toddlers. There were public schools in Massachusetts, but Nantucket had several different types of schools. The state government wanted to start public schools, but the Quakers, who formed the majority of the people living there, wanted to have their own type of education. Still, in 1818, the year Maria was born, Nantucket people had voted to have public schools.

Maria worried about going to dame school, though her mother said that the teacher who ran the private school for small children was clever and handsome. Her father gave her candy to encourage her, but Maria was determined not to read or write or do anything the teacher ordered.

On the first day of school, Mrs. Mitchell put on her best gray dress and her fine white kerchief and bonnet.

Maria herself wore a little gray frock. When they came into the teacher's parlor, the stout matron reached out her hand to Maria. She had a large nose, a larger chin, and little bright, sparkling eyes.

"I must leave now," Maria's mother said and walked toward the door. The teacher's fingers closed over Maria's hand and she pointed toward a little bench.

The child sat down reluctantly. When the dame said, "My dear, come here and read," Maria pretended not to hear.

When she repeated the command, Maria did not move. "Never mind," the teacher said, turning to the older girls. "She's just a baby. She'll be a better girl by and by."

"No, I shan't," said Maria, shaking her head.

"Here, come get this apple." The teacher held up a beautiful one as if she were going to toss it to Maria.

The little girl ran forward, holding out her apron, but when the teacher said, "You must read first," the child's face clouded, but she took the book and read one short sentence haltingly.

Later she had to learn by heart little stories about Adam and Eve and Daniel in the lion's den. Her mother had been a teacher and also librarian for a minister, but the only books for children at that time had frightening pictures.

In 1826, Admiral Isaac Coffin, a British subject, visited Nantucket with the idea of endowing a school there for the descendants of Tristram Coffin, his relative, who had been an early settler. He wanted to call it the Anglican School, but he was told that that would not be wise because there were not many Episcopalians on the island. There were six hundred children eligible to attend. Although eight-year-old Maria was related to Tristram Coffin, her parents preferred that she attend her father's private school. Later, she studied under her father in the first public school on Howard Street.

Her next school days were happy under Miss Elizabeth Gardner, a distant relative, who realized that Maria was shy as well as stubborn. Best of all, Maria liked her father's private school, for there the students and teachers took long walks over the moors, learning the names of plants and birds. She liked arithmetic there, too, because her father made up examples using the products of Nantucket and made the problems into a story.

When she was nine years old, Mr. Mitchell gave her lessons at home in beginners' algebra and some simple plane geometry. She always remembered one particular night when they were in the sitting room together and her father sat at his desk, proving that in an isosceles triangle, the angles opposite the equal sides are equal. Maria read, "An isosceles triangle is one with two equal sides."

She copied the drawing from the book and wrote: "To prove that Angle C equals Angle B, first draw line AD cutting Angle BAC into two equal parts and meeting BC at D.

"We know that AD equals AD (Axiom 1: Any quantity is equal to itself." That worked out in general she thought, looking down at her feet in their rough work shoes. Feet are more or less equal to each other.

"II. We know that AB equals AC because that was given in the hypothesis or first statement. We know that Angle DAB equals DAC because Axiom 4 says that halves of a quantity are equal to each other." She paused. "What right has the axiom to make a flat statement?"

Her father looked up and smiled. "Get an apple from the bowl in the kitchen."

She brought a rosy-cheeked apple to him and he cut it in half.

[25]

Maria's face lighted up. "Yes, I can see that they are equal." She went on with the rest of the problem and proved it to her father's satisfaction. It would always be characteristic of Maria to question and want proof.

Later, students met with Mr. Mitchell as friends and for mutual improvement in a public school on Howard Street. There Maria could learn without fear of punishment, and that was unusual in the early years of the nineteenth century. Whips were used in many schools.

When Maria was thirteen, she edited a little paper called *The Juvenile Inquirer* and wrote about her first school experiences, but she signed her article "Jane" so that people would not know who wrote it.

Her first reluctance about attending school disappeared with her father's teaching. She associated her lessons with home and with the sitting room, where she studied at night with Sally and the older children. She still missed Andrew, but his letters from the Sandwich Islands made the globe on her father's desk come alive.

She also spent many hours minding baby Eliza, talking to her and pointing out the colors of the roses on the wall in the sitting room and the bright minerals in the cabinet.

Near her third birthday, Eliza died from a throat ailment. That was Maria's first experience of sorrow.

When Eliza was buried in the plain Quaker burial ground, Maria could not bear to go there. It was the Friends' custom not to show pride with elaborate monuments, but surely little Eliza could have had a small stone inscribed with her name, Maria thought. She began to doubt the wisdom of some Friends' beliefs.

After school, Maria would hurry past the parlor, a place hard to bear since Eliza's funeral. She preferred to spend long hours in the kitchen, where there were many tasks to be done—washing dishes, filling the lamps with whale oil, and peeling fruits and vegetables.

[26]

When school was out for a month, Maria organized a little dame school in her own family garden for the toddlers and her cousins. The children liked geography best, for each one of them could claim a relative who had sailed to strange countries.

When Maria was fourteen, she realized the benefits of studying with her father. One autumn night in 1832, a year after the eclipse, Mr. Mitchell was absent on a coastal survey trip. Maria was studying in the kitchen, and the other children were gathered around the table, when the door opened and big Captain Bill Chadwick entered without knocking, as was the custom in Nantucket. With him the captain brought the fishy smell of whale oil, for he had just returned in his ship, the *Baltic*.

"Where's your husband?" he asked Lydia Mitchell holding out his chronometer. Maria knew that he wanted to have the instrument's rate corrected.

When Maria's mother explained her father's absence, the sea captain's face looked almost brutal as he turned away in disappointment. "Pity he couldn't be here when I needed him. Won't be back till Friday, you say, and I needs must pull anchor tomorrow morn."

"I'm sorry." Maria's mother explained that Rod Mason was usually available, but he'd gone to see a doctor on the mainland.

"But I've learned how to do it!" Maria blurted out.

"But is thee sure?" Her mother looked from her daughter to the visitor.

His face was unyielding. "Not a child like you." He looked down at the small, sturdy girl with the dark curls. "Should think you knew more about baby-tending."

The captain tightened his hold on the square box, but Maria reached out for it, looking directly into his eyes.

"I'll try ye," he said abruptly and handed over the chronometer.

As he closed the door behind him, Maria had a sudden wave of doubt. Could she really do it as her father did? Still, he had watched her do the whole process. Saying a little prayer inwardly, she put the captain's chronometer beside her father's.

That night Sally was more annoying than usual when they were doing the dishes. "Maria Mitchell thinks she's much, getting the captain's chronometer to fix!"

Maria did not answer the gibe, but her face flushed and her hand trembled as she hung the last mug on its hook.

Sally had made up a song: "Maria Mitchell, she's always a stickler."

Mrs. Mitchell came into the room at this point. "Stickler doesn't rhyme with Maria," she commented. "And it's rather a compliment to be called a stickler, for a stickler is careful about important things."

But when Sally's song became tiresome, Lydia Mitchell said, "Let dogs delight to bark and bite, but little children never."

Maria smiled. She and Sally were not little children, but they understood the message from the tone of their mother's voice. Sally stopped taunting and Maria closed the door into the garden.

She tried to occupy her mind with reading until the stars came out. Then she took a little table up to the roof. Later, she brought out a whale oil lamp, and then the chronometer, the sextant, and the telescope. She followed her father's directions exactly and turned the chronometer two points ahead.

Sometimes in the following nights she worried about the sea captain, but Bill Chadwick had no bad luck on his voyage, and he later complimented Mr. Mitchell on having a smart daughter.

Maria learned a great deal from teaching and having to explain to others, but she also was influenced by her cousin Walter Folger, whose library gave her a different type of knowledge. Abiah Folger, the mother of their distant cousin Benjamin Franklin, had lived on Nantucket Island. Like Franklin, Walter was an inventor, and he was an astronomer as well. One day, when the garden door to Walter's study stood open, Maria saw his astronomical clock. If only he would explain it to her! But Maria's mother had said that Cousin Walter was taciturn. When Maria had looked up that word in the Noah Webster dictionary, she had found that it meant "not given to conversation."

But she had heard him talk to the postmaster when he received interesting mail from Washington about his patents. When the mail boat came in, the whole town turned out. Maria followed along the next time, hoping that Cousin Walter would get some more interesting news and be less taciturn.

That day his mail included a magazine with pictures of the stars. She wished that she dared to ask him if she might borrow it. Then, perhaps, when she returned it, he might let her see the working of the wonderful clock. Walter's clock not only kept time and struck the hours but also showed the phases of the moon and the time of full tide at Nantucket Island.

Maria screwed up her courage as Mr. Folger turned in at his gate. "Good evening, Cousin Walter," she said. "When you've finished reading that magazine, could I borrow it? I'm interested in the stars." He looked so much like Benjamin Franklin that he might have been a brother instead of a cousin of the famous Pennsylvanian.

The short, fat man paused in surprise. "Interested in the stars . . . ," he repeated after her. Although she was only fourteen, she was nearly as tall as he. "Of course. I'll read it tonight. . . ." He paused, considering. "You might come for it tomorrow around four."

[29]

Maria was too excited even to tell her mother.

It was said that Cousin Walter would shut the study door and not even answer when his wife knocked. It would be terrible if he forgot all about telling her to come.

The next day she approached the door timidly and rapped on it twice. It opened wide. Cousin Walter pointed toward the clock! "You'll be interested in my invention. I hear you help your father when sea captains come in." He explained the clock in detail, and its calendar of the days, months, and year that changed at twelve o'clock on New Year's Eve, but she was even more interested in his reflecting telescope.

"You are really a wizard, like Cousin Ben Franklin," Maria said.

His eyes twinkled. "For that wise remark, I'll give you and your father the magazine to read; and later, when you need help from my books, you may read them. Just come in without knocking, and don't talk to me when I'm working at my inventions."

Maria looked at her cousin with awe. He was known to have corresponded with Thomas Jefferson, and Daniel Webster, who had served in Congress with him, had written that Walter ranked with the great discoverers in science.

Some of the books on astronomy and mathematics were too hard for Maria to understand at that time, but the corner table was a wonderful place to prepare her lessons. By that time she was attending the Young Ladies' School under the Reverend Cyrus Peirce, where discipline seemed to be more important than discussion. The schoolmaster had the air of a superior officer and not a friend, as her father had been. Later, appointed by the great educator Horace Mann, he headed the first normal school in the United States.

[30]

In the solitude of Cousin Walter's library Maria found help with her schoolwork. In addition to books on navigation, like *The New American Practical Navigator*, by Nathaniel Bowditch, she read stories of adventure and books of poetry. When she was sixteen, Eben Mason, a newcomer to Nantucket, came to Cousin Walter's house with her. Eben's dark eyes gleamed in his white face at the sight of the fine library. He was as much interested in astronomy as Maria was. Cousin Walter liked him and encouraged him to come often.

Eben and Maria liked to walk along the shore and on to the point called Tom Never's Head, where they could look at the breakers. Eben talked about going to Yale that fall, where he would study astronomy and advanced mathematics. He conjured up such glowing pictures of college life that Maria wished she could go too, and become a mathematics teacher.

"I wish there were a college for girls," Maria kept saying. "I'd like to be a teacher."

Eben smiled. "I believe there will be, someday, at Yale and Harvard. Girls are allowed to enter Oberlin College, I think. It's in the West, in Ohio . . . , but I don't know whether girls can enter all the classes."

"If only I could go," she said. "I wanted to go to sea, too, when Andrew went on the whaler."

"You wouldn't like it," Eben said. "You couldn't breathe in small quarters like that. A trip to Boston from here is enough for me."

"You're a landlubber!" gibed Maria. Strange that he liked to see the stars from land but not from shipboard!

In the autumn, Eben wrote to Maria from Yale about his work and a project he was working on that drew praise from his professors. Then his letters stopped. A classmate wrote Maria to tell her of Eben's death.

Trying to forget her sorrow, Maria worked harder

[31]

than ever. By that time she was an assistant to the Reverend Cyrus Peirce. She enjoyed teaching but was not happy under the minister's strict control. If Maria exclaimed at the sight of a rainbow, he frowned. He did not approve of discussion in the classroom.

Maria told her father, "I don't want to teach like Reverend Peirce. He won't even let us look out the window at a bird in a tree. I want to teach as thee does."

"Perhaps thee'll find a way," her father said. "Reverend Peirce has a better education than I have. I couldn't go to Harvard because my father lost money investing in a whaling ship. . . . I hope Andrew is all right. . . ." Andrew's second voyage was nearly at an end, and he had written that he was making port at Nantucket soon.

One morning the town crier called out, "Hear ye! Hear ye! Whale ship *Ann* hove in at Cape Cod! A fast schooner sighted her." Maria wakened the younger children and hurried downstairs.

"When will the *Ann* get here?" everyone asked.

"No telling," Mr. Mitchell said. "We'll go to the wharf." There was a great scrambling to get dressed and have breakfast. "Do you suppose we'll know him?" William Forster asked. "It's been a long time."

"I will," said Mrs. Mitchell. "He'll be asking for huckleberry pie!" She laughed. It was the first time since Eliza's death.

"We won't see much of him," Sally said. "He'll be looking for his girl. His last letter was all about buying a farm and settling down."

"You ought to know!" said Maria, for Sally, too, was soon to be married.

Sally's prophecy was right. When the *Ann* docked, Andrew put his arm around his mother and kissed everyone, but his eyes were not satisfied until he found his old sweetheart, Elizabeth Swain.

[32]

"Have you set the day?" Mr. Mitchell asked.

The bride-to-be blushed and Andrew said, "Soon."

When Maria returned to school, she decided that she did not want to keep on with her work as assistant, although the Reverend Peirce liked her work. She could sometimes become so absorbed in a problem that she would not hear him speak. He told others that Maria's mathematical ability was extraordinary. She considered herself slow, although very persistent.

3

What Good Is School?

Maria found it hard studying in the sitting room in the daytime, so her father suggested the little room at the foot of the attic stairs. She called it her cubbyhole. One side was bounded by the front window and the opposite side by the door. There were three shelves, and the lowest one became her desk. There she could spread out her papers to work on geometry and trigonometry problems.

Even though she hung out a DO NOT DISTURB sign, her younger brothers and sisters were constantly wanting her to take them for a walk or compose rhymes. She loved children and could not resist their pleading. They would pound on her door on rainy days saying, "Tell us a story." Phebe was afraid of thunderstorms, even though she was ten years old. Maria always let her come in and comforted her. She herself feared the sudden flashes and the growl of thunder.

On sunny days she went with them to the beach and entertained them by drawing pictures in the sand. She told them stories of Nantucket in rhyme and called it "my native isle."

When they were gathered in a circle on the beach one day, Maria sat on a log and recited a stanza about the sachem good and great who ruled over the Bay State.

"What's a sachem?" asked Phebe, who was in the third reader.

"A chief who heads a confederation of Indians," Maria said.

"What's a confederation?" her cousin Mary Brayton asked.

"Isn't it a group of Indian tribes joined together as the colonies were?" asked Ann, her auburn braids swinging with excitement. She was studying American history.

Maria nodded. "That's right, but maybe a little looser union. Some people said the story wasn't about a sachem but an Indian giant named Maushope, who liked to sleep on the sand on Cape Cod because the shape of it suited him."

"I know that story," said William Forster. "I heard it from a Mashee Indian who was captain of a ship that brought firewood to Nantucket from Cape Cod."

"Very well," said Maria. "Thee tell it."

"Well, this Indian giant or sachem slept badly," William Forster began. "He thrashed around a good deal and in the morning found that his moccasins were full of sand. First he took off one and then the other. Then he threw the contents into the ocean."

"And that's the way Nantucket and Martha's Vineyard were created," Maria said. "Nantucket means 'Faraway Island' in the Mashpee language."

The poems Maria composed for the children were later published in a little red book called *Seaweed from the Shores of Nantucket*. Maria wrote them down in her neat script and sewed the collection together.

Andrew was doing well with his own farm, and Sally had married Matthew Barney, a strict Quaker. Strange how Maria missed her, now that Sally lived at some distance from Vestal Street! They were such opposites, but Sally loved children as much as Maria did.

[35]

Having once started a dame school for little children in the garden, Maria began to think that she might start a real school of her own. Her father needed more money, because a partner in a whaling firm had defrauded him. The Mitchells had also welcomed a new baby named Eliza Catherine, called Kate, and Maria took charge of her because her mother had made a poor recovery. Mr. Mitchell was finding it hard to make both ends meet, for there were still six children in the family. He had become the secretary of the Phoenix Marine Insurance Company, but the settling of legal problems in shipping brought slow returns. He was often obliged to study lawbooks in the Atheneum Library, and Maria admired his persistence and his ability to educate himself by studying.

Every clear night during that summer of 1835, Maria went up to the sky walk with her father to study the changes in the stars. One evening she asked, "Does thee think I might teach, even if I'm only seventeen? Of course I had Reverend Peirce behind me when I assisted him."

"I taught when I was sixteen," her father said. "But I wore a beard, and I was a stranger to the pupils."

Maria laughed. "All I can do is wear longer skirts, and I stumble over them now. But I won't put up my hair, for even old ladies wear curls."

"Thee won't need to. I've seen thee teaching around here. Thee has a certain way with thee that will make students behave. Also, thee's good at explaining."

"The old Franklin School on Trader's Lane is vacant," Maria suggested.

"Why doesn't thee look into it? See if thee can rent one room," her father said.

The next day, Maria went to the Franklin School's caretaker, who was in charge of renting. She found that she could have one room free until the building was needed for an increased number of pupils in the public schools.

In her little study she composed an ad for the *Inquirer*. A school for girls would open September first at the Franklin School House on Trader's Lane. There would be classes in reading, spelling, geography, grammar, and history. Her nature lessons she called "natural philosophy." Then, arithmetic was important—geometry and algebra. The terms were three dollars a quarter, none admitted under six years of age. Her sisters Ann and Phebe enrolled.

On the first of September, Maria sat at a rickety desk facing rows of hard wooden benches. It was very quiet, and she heard only the foghorn. Would any pupils come?

Then she heard voices, and several girls from the white-pillared house on Main Street came into the room and sat down together on a bench, whispering and looking about critically. Soon some mild-mannered girls from the Friends' Meeting greeted Maria, and she answered, "How's thee today?" Next came three girls from "Little Egypt," the Portuguese fishing section. Two of them, wearing bright-colored sashes, had oval faces and olive complexions. The third was a little dark girl, who asked, "Can we come to your school? They won't let us go to the Free School on the hill."

Maria knew that there was opposition to colored children's attending that public school, although her father had had them in his public school classes when Maria was nine years old.

"Of course thee can stay!" Maria answered. The Quakers had long before approved equal education for all, male or female, white or dark. But the snippy older girls looked disdainful.

Maria explained to the children the Lancastrian sys-

[37]

tem, in which the older students taught the younger ones. The noise was terrific as the seniors, called monitors, were assigned younger students. One of the Quaker girls began to teach the little dark girl, and then the older ones stopped whispering.

Maria was tired that night. She was glad to have Ann's help in washing the dishes. After supper, she went up on the roof with her father.

"How was the school?" he asked. "Thee knows the first day is always the hardest!"

Maria knew that he was not feeling very well. He had found public school with older boys rather wearisome at times, but the Phoenix Marine Insurance position did not interest him as much as astronomy.

"It was good that so many came, but there was a little dark girl that I can't place," Maria answered.

"One of the Cooper children, I think," said her father.

"Oh, yes, I remember there was a story about a Cooper. . . . Thee said it happened when I was little."

Her father did not answer, for he was making a notation about a star's movement. When he had finished, he said, "Yes, Arthur Cooper was a slave from Virginia who escaped to Nantucket on a whaling ship about 1822."

"And his master came here to get him," Maria said. "Maybe this little Nelly is his youngest child."

"Could be. I had the older boys in public school. They signed on the crew of a whaler. I think Arthur has died. He married a Portuguese woman."

"The owner came with a police officer from Boston." Maria remembered the story well. "Arthur was living in a house down Egypt way."

"Some of the higher-ups in the Meeting engaged the owner in a discussion of a man's rights in front of Arthur's house," her father continued.

"And meanwhile, thee got him hidden in somebody's attic, and somebody else said he was lost in the subterranean passages of the moorland. What finally became of him?"

"Took ship for a while, and the owner returned to Virginia," her father said.

"Well, Nelly deserves to be in my school, regardless of what the proslavery people think."

Nelly Cooper showed her gratitude with a perfect attendance record.

For Maria's natural philosophy classes the children rose early to see the sunrise and watched how baby birds were hatched.

One day after geography, during a study period, Maria heard a singsong voice above the noisy sounds of teaching. Nancy Coleman, one of her distant cousins, was teasing the younger Pinkham girl by repeating a poor piece of doggerel about the early settlers.

"Since we're all related, you'd better come up and recite the poem for us all," Maria suggested.

Nancy Coleman came forward, her face so red that every freckle stood out. At first her voice was too low.

"Louder," said Maria. "Start with the second verse. Go ahead."

"The Rays and Russells coopers are," Nancy began.

> "The knowing Folgers lazy,
> A learned Coleman very rare,
> And scarce an honest Hussey."

"After all, Benjamin Franklin's mother was a Folger. You can't say he was lazy, and the verse lines are just as silly about the others," Maria interposed. "Now the next verse," she demanded.

[39]

"The Coffins, noisy, fractious, loud,
The silent Gardners plodding,
The Mitchells good, the Barkers proud,
The Macys eat the pudding."

"Mitchells aren't all good." Maria thought of their distant cousin, the wealthy Aaron Mitchell. He had been put out of the Meeting for making too much money, perhaps from smuggling in the War of 1812. Friends also disapproved of his having two houses, one much too fine, in town and another on the far shore, where illicit ships came in.

Someone tittered, and Maria took up the last line: "Obadiah Macy, the Quaker historian, does something besides eating pudding. Well! Go on!" said the teacher.

"The Swains are swinish, clownish called,
The Barnards very civil,
The Starbucks, they are loud to bawl,
The Pinkhams beat the devil."

"Now we'll find out why they say the Pinkhams beat the devil. Do you know?"

Mary Pinkham shook her head.

"My father has records of the Pinkhams before they came to Nantucket," Maria said. "They were in a Puritan settlement near Newburyport on the mainland. A great-great-great-grandfather of yours beat a drum to call the Puritans to be ready to fight the Indians. I suppose they thought the Indians were the devil in those days."

Mary Pinkham straightened up and looked proudly at the others as Nancy Coleman took her seat.

"Tomorrow, Nancy Coleman may bring a report from Obadiah Macy's new book on the history of Nantucket. We'll see why they decided to leave the mainland and live here." Maria handed the new book to Nancy, who took it eagerly.

[40]

Even though Maria simplified the algebra and geometry for the older pupils, they found the work difficult. They also complained about Latin as useless on Nantucket and said they didn't intend to go to the mainland. Maria's sister Ann was the only student interested in languages. Gradually the pupils dropped out for lack of money, and only a few faithful ones were left at the end of the last quarter before summer vacation. Her school could not continue.

Now Maria feared that she didn't know enough to teach, but she could not afford to go to college, as Eben had done. She hated to go to Cousin Walter Folger's library, because she missed Eben more when she was there. He had won an award in astronomy at college.

Mr. Mitchell was a member of the Atheneum Men's Library. Maria wished she had permission to go there. Then maybe she could study and teach better.

Sometimes she walked to Tom Never's Head to watch the breakers, or down to the wharves to count the ships coming in. Winter would be lonelier when the fog rolled in and her house was snowed in by blizzards. Then Nantucket really was a faraway island.

4

<hr/>

A Telescope and a Piano

The day her school closed, Maria returned home feeling completely discouraged. There seemed to be no future for her on the island.

She looked down at her drab dress and regretted the Friends' disapproval of bright colors. Her father had chosen bright, rich tones for the living room and even had his books bound in red.

As she reached home, she looked at the glowing colors of the flowers behind the white picket fence. If it was no sin to love them, why shouldn't people wear gay colors too? Maria agreed with the Friends' idea of the Inner Light, the Spirit moving them to act, and their abhorrence of war was certainly right. She felt she must talk to her father about the petty rules that worried her.

That night Mr. Mitchell was not home, however. There was a meeting of the Pacific National Bank officials. As Maria talked to Ann about her attending the public school that fall, she could not shake off her mood of depression. After the younger children had gone to bed, she went up to the roof walk and swept the sky with her father's little Dolland telescope.

It was comforting to locate the North Star. Then, sweeping farther, she saw Jupiter, but its satellites were obscured.

The summer dragged, even though Maria had a student in astronomy and navigation who wanted to qualify as mate on a whaling ship. He had worked up the ladder from cabin boy. She went to Walter Folger's house to study his astronomy books and Nathaniel Bowditch's navigation manual. Reading in translation Pierre Laplace's *Mécanique Céleste*, she was bemused by his theory that a great circular body of gas and dustlike nebulae had thrown out rings that had condensed and so formed planets like Jupiter, and even suns.

Later, when her father came up to the sky walk, she was looking at Jupiter. "Does thee believe Laplace's theory that the planets and the sun originated from nebulae?"

Her father shook his head. "It doesn't seem plausible, and I think it will be discredited."

After they came down to the sitting room, she said, "I wish thy Atheneum were open to the public."

The library had been started in 1820 by seven young men who later united with another organization and acquired a new building. Mr. Mitchell said that the Atheneum board was considering opening the library to the public. "They'll need a librarian, but I fear thee hasn't the qualifications."

"If only it were possible." Maria smiled ruefully.

Some weeks later, her father came into the sitting room with a twinkle in his eye. "How would thee like to be a librarian?" he asked.

"Well, I'm not sure, but I'd like to try," said Maria.

Her mother was smiling. "I think thee could do it. Tell her the good news, William."

"The Atheneum Association wants thee to be their librarian when the building is open, afternoons and twice a week at night."

"I'd love to do it, but will I get any salary?" Maria's forehead wrinkled.

"There'll be some remuneration," her father said. "The officers will tell thee about it tomorrow night."

She fumed and fretted the next day as she washed the interminable dishes, but at night a delegation from the Atheneum came to tell her that she could be librarian, beginning the following week, and would have a salary of sixty dollars the first year, seventy-five the second year, and a hundred finally.

Maria found the Atheneum's Doric columns imposing, but she felt dwarfed sitting in the spacious room behind a big desk. She learned that a lecture program was planned, with speakers from the mainland. As the ship-owners piled up fortunes, Nantucket was becoming one of the wealthiest towns in Massachusetts, and its citizens were interested in culture. They wanted to start a lyceum, bringing great speakers from Boston, and Maria found herself in the midst of the planning for the events, as well as advising young people on their reading and helping others in the evenings.

One night in 1836, William Mitchell came to the supper table with a happy expression. He had been appointed cashier of the Pacific National Bank at the head of Main Street. The bank was a beautiful building with pillars as magnificent as the Atheneum's.

"They want us to move there," he told his family, "and live in the spacious rooms upstairs."

There was surprise and consternation on the children's faces.

"Don't you want to live in the heart of the town?" Mr. Mitchell's voice held a note of surprise. "All Nantucket will pass below those windows."

"It's good for you to be cashier of the Pacific National Bank," said Maria.

"And have a salary of $1,200," her father added.

"But we do like this house," William Forster broke in. Francis, the quiet brother, said nothing.

"But this house is cozy and we've always lived here," Ann lamented.

"Ever since we were married . . . ," Mrs. Mitchell said. "But your father will have regular work . . ."

"We'll be nearer school," Phebe exclaimed, "and we can have our friends in for parties in the big rooms."

Maria tried to be cheerful, although she was not as much interested in parties as Ann and Phebe were. "Can we make observations on the roof?"

"Yes, we'll have a little wooden building on the roof and maybe two little houses behind the bank. Dr. Bache is trying to get us special apparatus, a new kind called a four-inch equatorial telescope." Mr. Mitchell was working under Dr. Alexander Bache on the government coast survey.

With Maria's help, William Mitchell built the little roof observatory, and eventually West Point lent them an altitude and azimuth circle. The azimuth circle was a necessary fitting for all compasses used for taking bearings—that is, noting the directions of objects on the earth or in the sky. The two small buildings behind the bank were for housing the transit equipment. William Bond, head of the Harvard Observatory, came to help them adjust the new instrument. Although he was the best-known American astronomer, he was a quiet, gentle person much like Maria's father.

Professor Elias Loomis arrived from Western Reserve College in Ohio and adjusted the transit instruments. The stump of a ship's mast was erected on the roof of the bank, and the azimuth circle was oriented to provide bearings on directions of stars and planets.

Maria and her father worked together. When the nip

of fall made viewing more difficult, she put on what she called "regimentals" and climbed "up scuttle" to the observatory. She wore a woolen hood, a heavy cloth coat, knitted socks, boots, and mittens. With eyes sensitive to changes in background and the pale light of stars and nebulae, she told her father what she saw and he recorded it by the light of the dim whale oil lamp. They recorded meridian altitudes to get time and latitude.

Once when Maria was alone and recording the time out loud, she heard a rattling sound. Then she saw two bright spots coming toward her, and something jumped on her lap. Her pet cat had come to visit the observatory.

There were other interruptions, once by a man who wanted Maria to explain what she was doing. But most of the time Maria was alone or working with her father. Sometimes they were rewarded in their hunt for a particularly difficult-to-see star.

Maria helped her mother with the housework in the morning and hurried to the library in the afternoon. She spent happy hours there, and sometimes she had free time to study. She helped sailors find reading and reference material while they waited for their ships, and they often came to see her again when they returned from their voyages. She saw them at the bank, too, where they brought their share from the sale of the cargoes. During that period of the great whaling fortunes, Nantucket banks outranked those of Boston and Salem in financial transactions.

William Mitchell was so busy with his bank job that he asked Maria to carry out his contract to execute a map of Nantucket. This made it necessary for her to travel from Madaket to Tom Never's Head. Maria found that the earth was almost as interesting as the stars.

While she was preoccupied with the map and the library, her sisters Ann and Phebe were being frustrated in their love of music. The girls were eager to have a piano, but Friends opposed the use of musical instruments on the grounds that they stirred up evil impulses.

Maria herself was tone-deaf and could not judge the musical quality of the piano, but she sympathized with her sisters and did not approve of restrictions on musical instruments.

The girls had obtained a piano but did not dare to have it brought into the house. It was put in the barn, because her parents knew that the Quaker Meeting would disapprove of such vanity, and if the piano should be discovered, they would be "dealt with" or "treated with," which were the expressions used then for the action of Meetings against such culprits. If the errant ones did not comply with the rulings, they were asked to leave the Meeting. A committee of one or more Friends would pay a visit to tell a strayer from the path of his offense, but if the Quakers were unsuccessful in convincing him of the error of his ways, several members of the Meeting would counsel with him. If the committee, too, was unsuccessful, he would have to appear before the Meeting. If he was unwilling to confess to his error, he would then be disowned.

On a cold day in the fall of 1838, Ann said, "We really should have the piano moved into the house. It will be ruined if it's out there during cold weather."

Since their father would be criticized if he paid for bringing in an instrument of evil, Maria offered to furnish the money from her savings.

It was arranged that Sally would invite the oldest Mitchells to tea. That would keep them away all afternoon, since Sally lived at some distance. Ann and Phebe arranged to have the piano moved to the upper hall, a pleasant room overlooking the square. The chronometers and books were kept there and it was the gathering place for their friends.

They decided to show the Quaker neighbors that their parents did not have previous knowledge of the piano. So, although the box was removed in the barn, the piano was moved down the street in broad daylight.

At the foot of the bank stairs, Maria stood ready to greet her parents when they returned from Sally's. Phebe was halfway up the stairs, waiting to give the signal for Ann to start playing. Kate stood by the piano. When their mother and father came to the door of the bank, Ann started to play "The Sailor's Tear," a mournful tune.

"What's this?" their father asked.

"Well," replied Maria, "we've had the piano moved in. I helped the girls with the payment."

Their mother was worried, but Mr. Mitchell rushed upstairs, delighted, and said, "Play something more lively!"

Then they all joined in singing, except Mrs. Mitchell.

The next day, a Friend and neighbor who was a Meeting official came to "deal with" Mr. Mitchell. He said he had heard from several people that Friend Mitchell had a piano.

Maria's father acceded that his daughters did have an instrument.

But, the Friend persisted, the piano was in Mr. Mitchell's house, and that was an offense against their Discipline.

"I do not wish my children to go away from their home for their pleasure. Besides, since I am the accredited financial agent of the Meeting, it might be improper for me to be under dealings," Mr. Mitchell suggested.

The Friend said, "Perhaps we'd better drop the matter. I'll speak to the rest of the committee."

Mr. Mitchell smiled when he told the girls of the old man's retreat, but the girls knew that their mother would not like them to consider the old man's discomfiture humorous. Lydia Mitchell could remember when her own father had been disowned by the Meeting for becoming a Freemason. To be expelled by the Meeting was a disgrace.

Maria's doubts began to pile up as she looked at the Friends' records that were in her father's possession but not generally available to the public. People confessed everything, from selling milk on First day, wearing bright buttons, and falling asleep in meeting for worship, to not using the plain language of "thee" and "thy" in their homes.

There were more serious offenses, like embarking on a ship that proved to be a privateer and carrying guns at the time of the American Revolution when Friends were supposed to be neutral and even sometimes favored England. Those who had fought in the Revolution were "cast out."

Also, a man who married an Episcopalian or a person of any other denomination was no longer a member, and his children had no birthright membership in the Society of Friends. If a man admitted his wrongdoing in marrying an outsider, all might be well, although the wife or husband of the confessor might not feel particularly pleased.

When Maria attended meeting, her doubts grew. Finally, two women representing the Meeting came to question her about her faith. According to their report to the men's section, Maria's mind was not steadfast on religious subjects and she did not wish to retain her birthright membership. She hoped that her mother would not be too unhappy when her case was submitted to the Monthly Meeting. Sally and her husband would probably be opposed to her action, but her other sisters, Ann and Phebe, would be sympathetic. William Forster and Francis were neutral. Maria was steadfast in her belief that the Spirit moved within each person, but tolerance and charity toward others was also important to her. She decided to attend the Unitarian Church, but she did not join the organization.

Although leaving the Friends was a drastic step, Maria's action drew her and her father closer together. There were factions within the Nantucket Meeting, and Mr. Mitchell followed the more outgoing Gurneyites. Neither he nor his daughter had been satisfied with the Nantucket Meeting. Father and daughter were very much alike. In their little observatory, the two of them worked together so closely that no one would be able to tell by their records where one left off and the other began.

5

———•◦❧◦•———

Fire!

Maria enjoyed her work at the Atheneum Library under the surveillance of Socrates, Plato, and Benjamin Franklin, whose busts stood on the tops of the bookcases. A larger room in the building was used for lectures, and a third spacious room contained an unusual collection. As Maria described it in an article she wrote for the *Nantucket Inquirer,* "There were documents of inestimable value, a rare collection of curiosities, works of man in his most barbarous state as well as most civilized." Some cabinets contained coins, minerals, and shells brought from Polynesia on whaling ships.

Through the Lyceum lectures, Maria came in contact with the greatest literary people and scientists of the first half of the nineteenth century. Professor Benjamin Silliman, the Yale University geologist and editor of his own journal, was a friend whose picture hung in the library.

One of the most interesting visitors, Maria thought, was Dr. William Bond, who had been her father's friend for many years. At his invitation, she visited the Harvard Observatory and his home in Cambridge, where she met his son, who bore a startling resemblance to Eben Mason. George Bond was tall for his age and slender, but his dark eyes met hers with the same understanding she remembered in Eben. George was seven years younger than Maria, and their friendship began in much the same way as her comradeship with students and sailor acquaintances in the library. Both were interested in astronomy.

Dr. Bond and George followed astronomical pursuits with Maria and her father. First news of the comet of 1843 came to the Pacific National Bank. Sailors from a whaling ship bringing in their lays, or shares of the cargo money, for deposit told Mr. Mitchell that they had seen the great comet in the South Atlantic Ocean. When it swept over the north, Maria and her father saw it in their little observatory and recorded its movements. "No wonder the Millerites think it brings the end of the world!" said Mr. Mitchell. "It's so bright!" That religious sect was predicting terrible events portended by the heavenly display.

Maria and her father viewed the comet with the Bonds in Cambridge, but messages from abroad indicated that the equipment at Harvard Observatory was inadequate. The work of the Bonds and Mitchells and some other astronomers stimulated so much interest that observatories were expanded in Cincinnati, at Harvard, and in Washington.

The next year, William H. Smyth's *Celestial Objects* was published, and George Bond began to study double stars. Following his observations, Maria was delighted with the beauty of their unusual colors.

George, whom she saw occasionally when visiting Cambridge with her father, seemed to her nearer Phebe's age than her own. Phebe had a talent for art, while Ann, who mastered languages easily, became a teacher in the public high school.

In 1844, one of Ann's students, Priscilla Haviland, invited Maria and Ann to come for a visit to Dutchess County, New York. They traveled by rail to Boston at the great speed of twelve miles per hour, then took the paddle-wheel steamer down the coast to New York City and up the Hudson River.

Although the two sisters were opposites in temperament and appearance, auburn-haired Ann was Maria's favorite sister. Ann was fastidious and interested in clothes, but Maria was indifferent to style.

The clifflike Palisades amazed the Nantucket girls, and they were interested in Tarrytown because of Washington Irving's writings. Poughkeepsie did not seem strange to them because there were some familiar whaling ships in port. The stagecoach ride to Priscilla Haviland's home seemed interminable after traveling on the new railway.

Maria saw the Friends' School that Lucretia Mott had attended. There was a great deal in the newspapers about Lucretia Mott. The former Nantucket resident was now active in the antislavery movement in Philadelphia. She had spoken at the Antislavery Convention in 1841 and later at the Nantucket Atheneum.

Maria was glad to get home to her quiet afternoons and the books on astronomy. Her knowledge of Latin from the Reverend Peirce's school helped her with her translation of *Theoria Motus Corporeum Coelestium* of Karl Friedrich Gauss, the great German astronomer, and she began to teach herself German, too, so she could read his other books. When she was reading *Gravitatem* by George Biddell Airy, Great Britain's astronomer royal, she felt friendly toward him because he had corresponded with her father. She also found a simpler edition of Bowditch's *The New American Practical Navigator,* containing additions by Professor Benjamin Peirce, a mathematics professor at Harvard who had been active in improving the observatory in Cambridge.

During the next years, Ralph Waldo Emerson, famous as an essayist and editor of *The United States Magazine,* had many speaking engagements in Nantucket and visited the Mitchells. Henry Thoreau, essayist, was on the Nantucket lecture program also, and John James Audubon, the authority on American birds, spoke there once. Another visitor was the noted physicist Joseph Henry.

Maria and her father were very much interested when the Smithsonian Institution opened in 1846. It was established with a grant from a British benefactor, James Smithson, for the "increase and diffusion of scientific knowledge in the United States." The Mitchells never missed an issue of the *Smithsonian Contributions to Knowledge*.

People came from the mainland to attend the Atheneum lectures, but Maria was busy at the library at the time the programs were scheduled. Housework was more difficult, because in the bank building the kitchen was on the ground floor. She noted in her diary that she sometimes put in a sixteen-hour day. Yet best of all she enjoyed the night observation, for she was glad to be working with her father.

One night in July 1846, Maria went to the Atheneum Library to advise a young student who was preparing to study astronomy at Harvard. As she was closing up her desk, he remarked, "Lieutenant Davis is in port with the Coast Guard ship."

"I knew they were coming soon," she said, locking the Atheneum door. Her father always invited the officers of the Coast Survey to their home. Maria especially enjoyed hearing the stories told by Lieutenant Charles H. Davis.

Although it was only a short distance from the Atheneum to the Pacific National Bank, she walked slowly that night. The air was sultry, as if a storm were brewing. After the long day, the stairs seemed harder than usual. She was glad to sink into the feather bed in her little room.

Suddenly she awoke. The clock was striking eleven and someone on the street was shouting, "Fire! Fire!" She hurried to the window and saw clouds of smoke.

"Where's the fire?" she called.

She heard her father's voice asking, "Which way?"

The answer was not clear. Maria dressed in a hurry and ran down to the portico of the bank, where her father was standing with Lieutenant Davis.

There were kegs nearby. "Is it powder?" she asked one of the men, but he was evasive. Her father said that Lieutenant Davis was ready to give the signal to blow up the powder. It might divert the course of the blaze.

Men, women, and boys were lined up, passing buckets of water and pouring it on the flames. Pushed about by the crowd, Maria found herself near the white-pillared Methodist Church. It was built of wood and would go up like tinder.

"Blow up the church and save the rest," someone ordered.

Maria could not bear to see the beautiful church go. She ran to the steps and stood there with her arms folded. "I dare thee to blow up the church!" she cried.

The men opening up the kegs hesitated. Then, as quickly as the emergency had arisen, it was over. Suddenly, the wind veered. The church and the bank were saved.

But the flying sparks caught the top of the little observatory. Mr. Mitchell, Maria, and Henry rushed to save the instruments. Although Henry was only sixteen, he was strong. The three of them took out the equipment and carried it into the bank for temporary shelter.

While they worked, however, the flames swept down

[55]

Centre Street to the Atheneum. The building burned to the ground. Its thousands of books and collections of coins, minerals, and shells were destroyed.

Afterward, Maria stood looking at the blackened ruin. Although the busts of famous people and many of the books and pictures had been removed to a safer place, the flames had reached them later, anyway. There was nothing left of the Atheneum.

At first, Maria could not believe that it was gone. She could not be sure, just then, that it would ever be rebuilt. Still, the situation was much grimmer for the people who had lost their homes and their working places. Banks, insurance companies, county offices, hotels, the Episcopal Church, and seven whale oil factories had burned. Worst of all was the destruction of provisions and medicines. One third of Nantucket Town had gone up in flames.

Although the two newspaper offices were burned, the owners set up temporary headquarters. The town selectmen sent out requests for help to Boston and other cities, and provisions poured in by ship.

The only things salvaged from the Atheneum Library were the portrait of Professor Benjamin Silliman, the great geologist, and a few books. The destruction of the Atheneum, the Coffin School Library, and private collections left the town without books.

Maria's father, as president of the Atheneum, called a meeting, and it was decided to use the library insurance money for the construction of a new building. Since he was authorized to send out circulars to other, similar institutions, Mr. Mitchell asked for duplicate books from their collections and for other help. Later, at Maria's suggestion, fifty shares of stock selling for as low as five dollars each were offered to complete the fund.

After the fire, Mr. Mitchell began the rebuilding of the observatory. Dr. Bond and George offered to help in adjusting the instruments. George, who had graduated from Harvard in 1845, had become his father's assistant in the Harvard Observatory, and he seemed more mature in appearance and outlook. He and Maria had much in common. Besides their interest in astronomy, they both loved nature and had a fine sensitivity to its beauty. Both were conscientious to a fault, and both overworked. At every chance, George came to Nantucket and Maria visited Cambridge.

On one of her visits, word had come by ship that the planet Neptune had been discovered. John Couch Adams, in England, had spotted it first, but Urbain Leverrier in France had received the credit. Professor Bond had looked for the planet as soon as he had heard the news, and he made observations again on the first night of Maria's visit.

His observatory was a little round building with a small telescope. He had drawn a map of a group of heavenly bodies, one of which he suspected was not a star but a planet.

George counted the seconds. The turning of the earth moved the stars across the field of view. If the points of light maintained the same relative positions as the night before, they must all be stars, but if any one of them had moved in relation to the others, it must be the planet Neptune. Dr. Bond looked at his son's record and said, "One of those stars has moved, and it's the one I saw last night. That is the planet!"

George and Maria each took a look. The glowing object looked like a small star. "What made you think last night that it was the new planet?" they asked.

Dr. Bond said simply, "I don't know. It was different from the others."

You cannot get a man of genius to explain steps, Maria thought to herself. He leaps to conclusions.

A year later, in May, Maria made a visit to Cambridge to see the new parts of the great refractor. She enjoyed going there, not only to make observations but to see George. He wrote her many times, urging her to come, and they were absorbed in their mutual enthusiasm for meteors, comets, and the moons of Jupiter. They obviously enjoyed each other's company.

6

Maria's Discovery

After six months, the Atheneum building was finished and Maria returned to her work. The town was gradually rebuilt, but it was never quite so prosperous again. The whale oil industry had been the basis of its wealth. The beautiful old houses of the shipowners lining Main Street testified to the gold that industry had brought.

Now, fewer ships were sailing to the distant whaling grounds. Railroads were taking people to settle the West. The ferryboat to the mainland was propelled by steam. Messages could be sent by telegraph.

Maria saw fewer sailors who were eager to learn how to navigate by the stars. Captain Thomas H. Sumner had published a pamphlet on a new way of obtaining the latitude and longitude of a ship, called the Sumner Position Line. Maria discussed it with her father, and he thought it the greatest step forward in the century as an aid to navigation.

The new Atheneum was a busy place for Maria. Her desk was in the center of the library room, and there she welcomed speakers for the antislavery movement, including Theodore Parker, minister and scholar, and Horace Greeley, publisher of the *New York Tribune*. Maria's friend Anna Gardner, from Nantucket, was also active in the abolition movement. The Atheneum auditorium upstairs was filled for the meetings. Maria knew that some of the Quakers and other residents of the town did not favor them but were not aggressive enough to try to break up the events as they had in 1841.

Maria and her father continued to watch the stars and search the sky for comets. Although she went back to writing a diary again, Maria put nothing personal in it. In the past, she had written of her happy days with Eben, and later about George Bond, and had seen the words burn up in the fireplace. Now she started a different type of diary, about the stars and her impressions of people and places.

On one page she commented that the aurora borealis was a pleasant companion. Faithfully, night after night, she made observations but she found no new stars. In March of 1847 she noted in her diary that she saw nebulae but that it was cold and her back was tired. Still she felt that seeing nebulae in new places made the vigil worthwhile.

On October 1, 1847, Maria's sisters were having a party in the big upper room, and Andrew and his wife had come in from the farm to visit, but they left early. Although Maria was tired, she crept up the attic stairs to the observatory to sweep the sky. Her little Dolland telescope seemed small since she had viewed the sky with the Harvard telescope.

In the upper part of the field that night she saw a blurry spot. Although she had become so familiar with that section of sky that she knew it as well as Main Street, she had never seen that spot before. She closed her eyes for a moment. When she opened them, the strange object was still fuzzy. Looking at the chronometer, she noted that the time was exactly ten thirty. Quickly she wrote the time in her notebook. Could this newcomer be a new star or a new comet?

Hurrying down the attic stairs, Maria heard the voices of the guests in the room below, but she must tell her father. Fortunately, he was seated near the parlor door. "Father, come up and look! There's a strange spot in the field."

Mr. Mitchell's face was alight with interest. He almost ran up the stairs behind her. But as he peered through the telescope, he said, "I'm not sure."

After shifting the lens, he scanned the field for a long time. Consulting the chart on the table, he said, "There never was a star or nebula in that place. It must be a new comet."

Turning to Maria, he put his arms around her. "It is a comet! Thee's discovered a comet above the North Star."

"Thee mustn't say it. It might be a star that we haven't followed. We'd better wait," Maria said, but she thought of George Bond and wanted to write to him.

Her father hurried to his desk in the next room. In the stillness, she heard the scratch of his pen. He was telling Dr. Bond, so there was no reason for Maria to write George.

The next morning there was a terrible storm, so the mail boat did not leave until October 4. When the rain and wind subsided and the sky was clear at night, Mr. Mitchell said, "I'm going up to see thy new comet."

"I'm not sure that it's my comet. The Bonds might have seen it first, or someone at the observatory in Ohio." Maria could not believe that she had really discovered it.

"A comet is named for the person who sees it first," her father said.

Soon a letter came from Dr. Bond with the message that he had followed Maria's reckoning and seen her comet. He had sent the information to the Hamburg Observatory in Germany.

There was a letter to Maria from George on October 20. When she saw his name on the envelope, she went up to the observatory so that she could be alone to read it.

> Cambridge, October 20, 1847
>
> Dear Maria:
>
> *There, I think that is a very amiable beginning, considering the way I have been treated by you. If you are going to find any more comets, can you not wait until they are announced by the proper authorities? At least don't kidnap such as this last.*
>
> *If my object were to make you fear and tremble, I should tell you that on the evening of the twentieth I was sweeping within a few degrees of your prize. I merely throw out the hint for what it is worth.*
>
> *It has been very interesting to watch the motion of this comet among the stars with the great refractor; we could almost see it move.*
>
> *On account of the passage over the star mentioned by your father, when he was here, it could make an interesting notice for one of the foreign journals, which we would readily forward.*
>
> Respectfully,
> Your obedient servant,
> G. P. Bond

So George might have discovered the comet first, Maria thought. Was he just joking, or did he wish that he had found it first? Maria put aside doubt. George was always generous. Anyway, someone in Europe might have seen the comet first.

Her father had voiced the same thought when he went

to Cambridge to see the comet through the refractor. Maria wished she could have gone, but her mother was confined to her room with an illness the doctor could not define.

In 1831, King Frederick VI of Denmark had offered a gold medal valued at twenty ducats to be awarded to the first person discovering a telescopic comet. The king stipulated that the award should be given to the first person who wrote in by the first post after the discovery. Since Frederick VI had died, his son would make good his father's promise, but the finder had to report to the nearest qualified observatory at once to have the discovery verified.

The Mitchells had complied with the requirements, since Dr. Bond was head of the nearest observatory, but the letter had not left Nantucket until October 4 because of the storm. The announcement of the discovery had been delayed three critical days.

Early in November, a letter arrived from Dr. Bond in the bank mail, and Maria's father was so excited that he brought it to her in the kitchen, where she was preparing her mother's meal. "The comet hasn't been seen in Europe!" he said.

Maria could not speak. There were tears in her eyes. "I can't believe it!" she said.

Her father told her that a ship had come in from Hamburg with the news.

"I was afraid that someone might have seen it first. Then I did discover the comet! That is the greatest day of my life—October first, eighteen forty-seven."

Then letters arrived telling of the comet's being seen by Father de Vicco at the observatory in Rome on October 3, by W. R. Dawes at Kent, England, on October 7, and by Madam Runker, the wife of the director of the Hamburg Observatory, on October 11.

[63]

Maria's heart sank at the news. The possibility of the award's being snatched away when it seemed so near was almost more than she could bear. Dr. Bond and the Honorable Edward Everett, president of Harvard College, wrote to George Biddell Airy, astronomer royal of Great Britain, and to the American minister in Denmark as well, about the cause of the delay. Maria Mitchell's name as winner of the award was brought to the attention of the king of Denmark.

Meanwhile, she went ahead with her usual tasks at home and in the library. Her mother could barely walk and needed the help of Maria and Kate. Ann and Phebe were teaching, while Henry was with the Coast Survey. William Forster and Francis were working outside the Nantucket area.

A year went by. The few sailors who came in to get books complained of the scarcity of whales and the decrease in the number of ships sailing to distant ports. Most of the old whaling ships had been family investments and the crews had been related to the captains, but now riffraff came in from other ports, and there was talk of cruelty and mutinies.

More and more young men were leaving the island for the mainland every year. Even older people, such as Maria's uncle Isaac Brayton, were talking of going to Ohio to live. Of course there were still people who said, "I never want to go beyond Sankaty's light and I'll live and die within sound of harbor bells."

Maria grew restless. She wanted to go beyond the shoals and Buzzards Bay into the world beyond. Commander Davis, who had worked with the Coast Survey and had helped the town in the Great Fire, was interested in founding a new almanac in Cambridge, the *American Ephemeris and Nautical Almanac,* sometimes to be called the *Harvard Almanac.* He hoped to find Maria a place on the staff, although no one had ever heard of a woman computing data for an almanac. Maybe Maria would be considered more seriously by the *Ephemeris* board if she received the medal. Somehow, as the weeks dragged on, that seemed less possible all the time.

One day in the fall of 1848, when Maria and her father went to the post office as usual, the nervous clerk thrust a letter into Mr. Mitchell's hand that he had known was addressed to Maria.

"It's for thee," her father said. It bore the return address of the Danish minister in Washington, and it displayed the large red seal of the king of Denmark. Perhaps they were just letting her down with a kind letter, Maria thought.

She tore it open determinedly and glanced down the page. "They have given me the award," she announced.

But she could not quite believe it until a package was forwarded to her from Washington. That time she hurried home from the post office and up to her own room before opening it, her hand trembling a little.

Inside was the gold medal. On one side, in Latin, was engraved "Christian, King of the Danes," and on the other side she translated, "Not in vain do we watch the setting and the rising of the stars."

She liked that. Her study of the stars had been worthwhile. Below that inscription was "Comet seen," and the date "October first, 1847." Around the edge in large letters, under "comet," was printed "Maria Mitchell." She was not only the first American to see the comet, but also the first woman in the world to have a comet named for her.

A famous astronomy journal had a whole chapter on "Miss Mitchell's Comet." Maria laughed about being a celebrity in Boston, but she did enjoy sending a short article on her discovery to the new Smithsonian Institution in Washington. The director, Joseph Henry, sent her an award of one hundred dollars. That thrilled her almost as much as the king's medal, for it represented recognition from a scientific organization. Later, Henry became one of Maria's friends, and she considered that gift one of the three great influences in her life.

Maria was the first woman to be elected to the American Academy of Arts and Sciences. Two years later, through the influence of Louis Agassiz, the great professor of botany and zoology at Harvard, Maria was unanimously accepted as a member and asked to join the American Association for the Advancement of Science.

Her reception by scientific organizations in New York and Boston was exhilarating, but the sudden interest of wealthy people that followed only amused her. She was happy to return to her observatory on top of the Pacific National Bank Building.

Through the good offices of Commander Davis, Maria was appointed a computer on the staff of the *American Ephemeris and Nautical Almanac* at three hundred dollars a year, a salary that seemed enormous to her for doing the work she loved. Later, there were times when the computing was difficult. She wrote in her diary that her letter from Commander Davis had come and she had had to revise some work, but by shutting herself up all day in her little room she had gotten it done. It was a satisfaction to know that the computations in the almanac did simplify navigation.

Now all the world seemed to be coming to Maria's library. She never forgot the children who asked for adventure books, often recommending the books of Herman Melville and Edgar Allan Poe's *The Narrative of Arthur Gordon Pym,* but she did weary of the people who considered a woman astronomer an oddity.

In every mail there were letters from George—notes about the telescope at Harvard, notes on stars and comets. There is nothing in Maria's diary to prove it, but people of the time said later that Maria and George were deeply in love.

7

Love Denied

One afternoon in 1848, Maria picked up her copy of the *New York Tribune* at the post office and took it to the Atheneum. Since there were no visitors, she unrolled it to read and found on the front page the name of her friend and distant cousin Lucretia Coffin Mott in a news story about the first women's rights convention in Seneca Falls, New York. The women, meeting at the home of Elizabeth Cady Stanton, had decided that their chief goal was votes for women. Maria herself, although in favor of suffrage, wished even more that women could have the right to education. That was her own personal priority.

The article also mentioned Susan B. Anthony, who had been a speaker for women's legal and social rights. Mrs. Anthony, a teacher, said that women's pay should be equal to that of men.

After visiting cities on the mainland, Maria realized that Nantucket women were more independent than most. Perhaps it was because their husbands were away for months, sometimes years, on whaling vessels. If women had equal rights, she, Maria, could have gone along as a sailor when Andrew had sailed away with Uncle Isaac, so long ago.

Maria thought about the problem again when Andrew's wife said that he was tired of farming and wanted to go west. Soon after that, everyone was excited over the discovery of gold at Sutter's Mill in California.

One cold night in January 1849, Maria was working at her computing assignment in her room when there was a loud rap on her door. She opened it to find Andrew with the *Nantucket Inquirer* in his hand. She had not seen much of him since she had discovered the comet.

"Have you seen this?" He pointed to an advertisement that read, "Boots for hunting gold in California."

Maria read the notice and laughed. "I doubt that you'd find more gold by wearing them."

"A lot of my friends are going," he said. "I'm sailing on the *Aurora* for California."

"Oh, I wish I could go!" Maria said. "Remember how I wanted to go with you so long ago?"

"This will be just as hard sailing," Andrew said. "We'll go around Cape Horn."

"Oh, I know I can't go," Maria said with a sigh, "but I wish I knew what's best for me to do. I can't stay in the library always. Of course the summers are the worst, with all those people asking silly questions about my discovering the comet."

Andrew tried to show enthusiasm, but he had never shared his family's interest in astronomy. Ships and tides were his life.

Although Maria envied Andrew's trip to California, she was absorbed in her work. The next year, she was delighted to receive an invitation from Dr. Bache of the Coast Survey to come to the observatory in Independence, Maine, as an employee. Her young brother Henry was also invited. They would be taught the use of the zenith sector and the zenith telescope, which would be much easier than using the awkward prime vertical transit that Dr. Bache had helped them install on top of the bank nearly fifteen years before. Astronomical instruments were improving, and now Maria could complete an observation in a few minutes.

The summer in Maine was one of the high points in her life. The peaceful setting and interesting work made the experience nearly perfect.

Back home again in Nantucket, she found time in her busy schedule of library duty, housework, and computing to help her sister Phebe inspect rooms on Main Street that might be suitable for an art school. Kate, now fourteen, decided to enroll. She had begun to wear her hair in a knot and looked like a young model from *Godey's Lady's Book.*

Maria, now thirty-one, still wore her black hair in curls. She considered herself homely, but respected her own worth. She was discouraged when *Godey's* editor, Mrs. Sarah Josepha Hale, wrote asking Mr. Mitchell for a short paper on Maria's literary and scientific endeavors. "She might at least have written me direct," Maria said.

But she did enjoy Ralph Waldo Emerson's including her in an article on "Female Astronomers" in his *United States Magazine.* He wished that Maria would give science lectures, but somehow she could not make up her mind to speak on the lecture platform.

Another disconcerting experience came two years later, when an artist named Hermione Dassel wrote requesting permission to paint a portrait of Miss Mitchell with her father. Maria started to write a letter of refusal but then decided that that would be discourteous.

When Maria came down into the living room on the fateful night, she found Kate sitting by the table sewing. Kate wore her hair parted in the middle, and the simplicity of her coiffure emphasized her regular features. "If only you'd let Mrs. Dassel paint you instead of me!" Maria said. "After all, you look older than sixteen."

"But she wants to paint you because you are famous.

That wouldn't be right." Kate was shocked at the idea.

"You could look through the little telescope just as I did when I discovered my comet."

"It would be wrong!" Kate insisted.

When her father came in, Maria told him the problem.

"You ought to go ahead yourself," her father said.

"Why don't you pose with Kate?" Maria suggested. "You are the real astronomer."

When Mrs. Dassel came, she finally decided to paint Kate looking into the little Dolland telescope and her father sweeping the sky with the larger one. Maria later allowed drawings and photographs of herself, but she always disliked having pictures taken, so most of them were unsuccessful.

Maria had reached a crossroads. George Bond wanted a definite answer to his proposal of marriage.

"I am seven years older than you," Maria told him. They were up in the observatory over the bank.

"Seven years doesn't make any difference," George insisted. "Loving each other and being interested in the same things is more important."

"But I look older."

"That isn't true."

While he was talking, Maria could not help believing that they could work out a happy life together. But later, at home alone, she was not so sure. She was afraid that the difference in their ages would matter more as they grew older, so she suggested that they stop seeing each other.

After George left, there was an emptiness in her life that she tried vainly to fill with the library and the stars.

During that period, a number of noted speakers appeared at the Atheneum, including abolitionists Josiah Quincy, Theodore Parker, and William Ellery Channing and suffragists Lucy Stone and Elizabeth Oakes Smith. In

1852, Herman Melville visited Nantucket and spent an evening with the Mitchells. Maria enjoyed the stimulating contacts, but they could not replace her friendship with George.

Then she heard that George was engaged to Harriet Gardner Harris, a distant cousin of hers about George's age. Somehow that news changed everything. Maria had not expected him to react to her suggestion so quickly or in such a way, although she had thought his interest in her might taper off. Now she missed his frequent letters and her life lacked zest.

She busied herself attending meetings with her father in Boston and writing in her diary about the scientists she met. She was truly happy when George reported making the first daguerreotype of the moon with the new refracting telescope at Harvard. That was the first step in another astronomical revolution and the beginning of George's continuing experimentation with photography of the stars.

Maria did not like summers on Nantucket because of the invasion of tourists. They did bring money to the island, but Maria preferred the prosperity of the whaling industry. She also hated to be pointed out as a famous phenomenon, Exhibit A in the astronomy world of Nantucket. She wanted to substitute someone else at the Atheneum and get away from the silly questions.

But Maria always enjoyed a good laugh, especially at her own expense. An episode occurred at Ann's wedding that amused her. The auburn-haired sister was marrying Alfred Macy of Nantucket and the family made great preparations. Distant relatives and some mainlanders were invited. For additional help in the kitchen, Nelly Cooper, Maria's former student, brought a new girl from the fishing village whose hair was as black as Maria's own. "She's not Portuguese like my mother, nor from

the Azores," said Nelly. "She's from Jamaica Island."
The new girl curtsied like a well-brought-up young lady.

"Can she serve?" asked Maria.

"Yessum," said Nelly. "She works in the clam bar. My brother calls her the Queen's Waitress because Jamaica is English-owned."

"I'm sorry you couldn't get someone we've had before, but you can help her," said Maria. She hurried to the front of the house.

Phebe was already meeting guests at the door, and the Jamaican might be able to help Nelly. "Tell her about the kitchen," Maria said hastily.

Kate seated herself at the piano and played a lively tune for guests who were already seated. A large, fat woman was struggling up the stairs with a distant cousin of Maria's in her wake. "Which one got the gold piece?" asked the fat guest. "The one the king sent her."

Maria dodged around the corner. The fat woman's eyes lighted on the Jamaican girl, who was nearby, and she said loudly, "So this is our famous Maria."

The frightened new girl said, "Oh, I'm not the famous lady," and she hurried down the stairs. The upper hall was full of people.

"But you said she was the darkest of them all," the large woman insisted.

"Yes, but not that dark," said the cousin, "and homelier."

Maria smiled ruefully as she slid behind a tall man. Then she went to the kitchen to help with the raspberry shrub and to unwrap a ship's model, the wedding gift of college friends in Boston.

When the simple ceremony was over and the newly-weds were to be driven to the ferry dock, Maria was too tired to go with the family. She said, "I'll help Mother get ready for bed." She wasn't superstitious, but it would

[73]

make her sad to see Ann disappearing into the fog. Of course she would be returning to Nantucket to make her home there, but it would not be the same.

Mrs. Mitchell was becoming more difficult to care for as she became more absentminded, and she had to be watched over like a child. Later in the year, Phebe and Kate agreed to stay at home so that Maria could go on a short trip to New York and Washington.

Maria felt that she, too, might leave the island for a while to renew her friendships on the mainland and get a different outlook. She had hired Bridget, a young Irish woman, to help at home. Phebe was in charge of art classes until the spring, when she would be married and go away with her husband, a professor in a theological seminary. Since Kate would soon be going to Boston for classes, Maria thought it would be a good time for her to take a breather.

In New York, Maria met Horace Greeley again. Mrs. Dassel entertained for her in Washington. She saw her friend Dr. Bache and the brave Dorothy Dix, who had told Congress of the horrible conditions in insane asylums. At the Smithsonian she met and talked with its director, Joseph Henry, who had encouraged her with the award of money when she had discovered her comet.

She realized more forcefully than before that women on the mainland were not so independent as those on Nantucket. Her friend and distant cousin Lucretia Mott was ridiculed for her stand on women's rights at Seneca Falls. Maria read Dr. Hall's book *The Life of Mary Ware* and disliked the emphasis on sewing as the universal occupation of women. Too much attention to sewing and cooking could shut out the study of the universe, she knew.

Back in her Atheneum library room in November 1854, Maria had an opportunity to talk with James Freeman Clarke, the biographer of Margaret Fuller, whom she very much admired.

It seemed to Maria that 1855 was the hardest year of her life. Her mother was very ill, and several friends died. George Bond no longer came to visit, although they still corresponded. He gave Maria some advice about repairing the threads in her transit instrument with spider webs.

Finding gray threads in her hair, Maria determinedly pulled them out.

She had saved enough money to go abroad, but her friends were horrified at the idea of her going alone. Commander Davis told her that he could not advise her going at that time, for there might be changes on the staff of the *Harvard Almanac.* So she became a prisoner on Nantucket through the hard winter of 1857.

The harbor was frozen over from January 5 that year. People did not mind at first, for they all went sleighing, but that was no longer fun when the weather grew colder. High winds and blinding snowstorms kept everyone inside. Maria's father shoveled snow from the observatory and said that everything got a good washing.

When a ship was sighted off Siasconset, the Mitchells drove over to see it. Maria wrote in her diary that even though they were Christians, the hard-up natives dreamed of what might be salvaged if the ship ran aground at Nantucket. The women were picturing the silks that might be aboard, and the men talked of the wreck agents' fees.

The ship did signal for a pilot, and a Nantucket man went out in a dory, returning with word that the ship needed provisions. She was from Glasgow, en route to New York. Food was brought from Nantucket, and the ship disappeared in the fog.

There were seven hundred barrels of flour left in the

town, but fresh meat was getting scarce. Supplying the ship had depleted the stores. The poor Irish were lacking provisions, so Maria's mother suggested giving food to Bridget. This had been her first sign of interest in events around her for a long time.

When the roads were impassable, the Mitchell girls met with friends nearby. During interminable days without mail or newspapers, the family resigned itself to the continued blizzard. Phebe and Kate, both engaged to be married, bore up without letters from their fiancés. Kate was twenty-one, but her future husband was much older. Owen Dame was a strict Quaker who had lived in Chicago. They expected to live in Lynn, Massachusetts. Maria would miss having her little sister nearby.

Kate and Maria decided to kill time by learning poetry during the snowstorm, but it was hard memorizing the dull parts of Oliver Goldsmith's "The Deserted Village," and John Greenleaf Whitter's "Snow-Bound" was too close to their own experience. They organized a club, with three meetings a week, to compose poetry. Maria's new copy of Elizabeth Barrett Browning's *Aurora Leigh* went the rounds of the neighborhood.

Unfortunately, Maria could not receive her assignments for the *Harvard Almanac,* and because of the cloudy weather she could not make observations in the little building above the bank. Even her customary patience was tested to the breaking point. Her dreams of traveling in the world seemed hopeless.

At last, on February 5, after being shut in by storms for a month, Maria went to the post office, eager for the mail. There was her usual assignment from the *Harvard Almanac* and there were some magazines, and down in the back of the box was an official-looking letter from General H. K. Swift of Chicago. Possibly someone wanted her to talk about her comet. She realized that she was

[76]

getting in a rut in the small world of Nantucket. She decided to keep the letter until she reached home, for snow was beginning to fall again.

In her hurry, Maria passed by several young women she knew without saying hello as she usually did. I am losing touch with students at the library, she thought I must have them over for a taffy pull and show them the stars through my telescope. But of course her mother should not be disturbed.

When Maria reached home, Mrs. Mitchell was asleep in the four-poster bed. Maria shut the blinds and put a tumblerful of spring water on the little table. Then she left the door open to her own room so that she could hear her mother call if she needed medicine for her rheumatic pain.

Maria pulled her rocking chair to the window, but the wintry sky was dark now. She had to light the whale oil lamp. By its yellow glow Maria saw from the letterhead that General Swift was a banker in Chicago. To her amazement, she found that he was asking her to chaperone his seventeen-year-old daughter, Prudence, on trips to the southern states and to Europe. He wanted the girl to have the advantages of travel and the study of elementary science, and he thought that Maria would be an interesting companion. She could decide on the most educational places to visit. All expenses would be paid by General Swift!

If Maria took the offer, she could meet interesting people in their own homes and see great observatories. She could teach again, instead of being an exhibit at the Atheneum Library.

"Prudence" sounded so solemn. . . . Why not call her young companion "Prue"? Then again, the girl might have romantic ideas and be hard to handle in a foreign land. . . . More likely, though, Prue would be timid about being on shipboard. . . . Suppose there was a shipwreck and they had to be transferred to another steamboat?

Maria remembered Andrew telling stories of leaving a foundered ship by a narrow plank placed from the deck to another vessel. Shutting her eyes, Maria pictured the scene and knew that she was timid herself and would be afraid to walk a plank. Usually she put up a brave front, as she had during the town fire when she had ordered Lieutenant Davis' men not to blow up the Methodist Church. He had said afterward that he had noticed her for the first time that night.

Of course, if she took the trip with Prudence Swift, she might lose her salary from the *Harvard Almanac*. Besides, she was needed at home, for her mother's condition, after a six-year illness, was worsening. Phebe would soon marry Joshua Kendall. Henry was advancing in the Coast Survey, and William Forster and Francis were working. None of them was able to take care of her mother as Maria did. She really couldn't accept General Swift's offer to be a guardian to his daughter, she thought. In her mind she pictured Prudence Swift as a willowy blonde with golden curls who would never venture to coast downhill or go out on the shore in a windstorm. She would not be like the Nantucket girls Maria had taught. Being Prudence's guardian angel might be difficult.

Outside the window, the bare branches had stopped swaying. Maria decided to go down on the beach and walk. Perhaps she could decide about General Swift's offer if her head was clear. She put on a worn reefer and some old pants of Henry's. As she walked along the shore, she tried not to be selfish and to think of her duty to her mother. She reminded herself that all the members of the family had a good reason for studying or working where they wished.

8

❧

In Distinguished Company

While Maria went on with her usual routine in February 1857, Sally decided that she could manage to care for their mother with the help of an aunt. Then Commander Davis of the *Harvard Almanac* agreed to permit Maria to take her data away on a voyage and do her computing abroad. So Maria accepted General Swift's offer and began to prepare for a tour of the southern states with joyous anticipation.

Setting out for Chicago later that month, Maria heard much discussion on the train as to whether Kansas Territory would become a free or a slave state. The Dred Scott decision complicated the matter, for that decree gave an owner the right to bring back an escaped slave from a state where slavery did not exist.

Nantucket was a stop on the Underground Railroad for slaves escaping to Canada and freedom. Quakers had protested the practice of slavery for many years, though not all were abolitionists. Maria knew that her father believed that no man had a right to own another and that the Nantucket slave Arthur Cooper had deserved his liberty. Perhaps they would see slaves on the trip. The new development was like a cloud obscuring the happy prospect of her tour.

In Nantucket she had attended the Antislavery Convention led by her abolitionist friend Anna Gardner and her cousin Lucretia Mott. There she had heard Frederick Douglass plead for freedom and equality for the slaves. She wondered again what kind of girl she would be accompanying on this southern trip. The general would be with them for some part of the journey. Would they both be proslavery?

A few days later, Maria's hansom cab drew up before the Swifts' home in Chicago. As a maid in uniform opened the door, Maria heard someone crying. Could that be Prudence or some child?

"She's spoiled," the maid explained. "She wants her father to go all the way on the trip. She doesn't want you to go as a chaperone."

"She hasn't even seen me!" Maria tossed back her curls as she had when the sea captain said that she was too young to test the chronometer. "She'll have to get used to me."

"She'll be better when her father comes home from a business trip. I'll show you to your room so that you can freshen up for tea at four. Prudence will come down to meet you, I hope." The maid added the last two words dubiously.

In the bedroom, Maria saw by the French clock that it was three forty-five, leaving time only for washing her face and brushing her hair. Prudence could think what she pleased.

In a parlor crowded with heavy furniture, Maria found a dumpling of a girl seated behind a tea table.

"Good afternoon, Miss Maria." The girl drew out the long "i" in Maria. "How do you take your tea?"

"As it pours," said Maria, "and no sugar."

"I take mine for the sugar," Prudence said. "Daddy is so mean. He wants me to get thinner. He's really cruel, cutting down on the sugar." She pouted, but Maria saw that her mouth was well shaped. The girl would have been pretty if she hadn't stuck out her full lips.

"I'll call you Prue if you'll call me Maria with a long 'e' sound," Maria offered.

Prudence smiled. "I like Prue better, if Daddy doesn't object to a nickname."

Maria saw that she had made a step forward in their relationship.

General Swift, a gracious older man, returned that night, and Prue was on good behavior during the trip to St. Louis. She even seemed mildly interested when Maria saved a candle to use later for smoking glass when there was an eclipse. "We'll have this ready, for the eclipse will take place when we are on shipboard," Maria said. "We won't hurt our eyes looking at it."

Prue made a little face as she looked at the black from the candle on Maria's finger, but she seemed to like Maria better now and bade her father farewell without protesting too much.

"I hope you'll explain advances in science in the nineteenth century," General Swift suggested. Maria nodded reassuringly, remembering her father's conversations about their own times.

Prue seemed excited by the ship *Magnolia* and the handsome captain. She and Maria enjoyed the leisurely glide down the Mississippi River. When they were five hours from St. Louis, they came into the dining room and were seated in the places of honored guests.

On the second night, Maria felt a queer shivering motion of the boat. The captain sighed and said, "We're touching bottom. It's a sandbar."

Prue turned white.

"Must we wait for the incoming tide?" asked Maria, thinking of fishing boats grounded near Nantucket.

"There isn't any tide on this part of the river," the

captain replied glumly. He excused himself and hurried forward.

Prue pushed away her dessert and began to crumble bread nervously.

"When I have finished my coffee, we'll go on deck," Maria said calmly, and in a minute or two they went outside. They were quite near land, and the steward said that they would soon be put ashore. The captain had ordered a small boat lowered to sound the depth.

"Shallow water ahead and on the right and left," a sailor reported. "It's not a fit place for landing."

By two o'clock they were still high and dry. The helmsman was moving the ship cautiously. There was a tremulous motion. "Let's sit here and go on reading *As You Like It,*" Maria suggested. While they took turns, the time passed until they went to their spacious cabins. It seemed to Maria that Prue was trying desperately to be composed.

That night Maria closed the porthole over her bunk, glad to shut out the night. She wished she were in a cozy room in Nantucket. I'm really homesick, she thought.

The next day the ship was on the same spot. Maria and Prue continued with their Shakespeare reading. The day was uneventful, except that another ship stopped on the sandbar near them, and they went up to the wheelhouse for a better view. The captain sent up oranges with his compliments.

The next day Prue was getting restive, but Maria calmly encouraged her to read and to write letters. For two more days they were aground. Maria began to think that the *Magnolia* would stay on the bar until the ship petrified, but she kept a brave face before her companion.

On the fourth day they left the *Magnolia* in a rowboat to reach the smaller steamer, the *Woodruff.* Prue and

Maria held hands when their little boat swerved as if it were going under the *Woodruff.*

Aboard and moving again at last, they arrived in Cairo, Kentucky, the next morning. There were cherry blossoms on shore, for spring had come on the twenty-fourth of March. Maria remembered the eclipse and brought out the candle she had taken from the hotel in St. Louis. Holding a piece of blackened glass from a broken window of the *Magnolia,* Prue saw her first eclipse as Maria had so long ago. This time the sky was cloudy and the sun had bars across its face.

Their boat stopped at a coal landing called Madrid, was temporarily delayed the next night, when its paddle wheels were snagged, and reached Natchez the next morning. In a few days they had arrived in New Orleans, a city that terrified Maria. The strange people talking a strange language made her long for quiet Nantucket and its harbor bells. Then she thought, It's a little like the sound of the Portuguese language on Nantucket. Prue began taking more interest in studying French, in order to be ready for Paris.

Despite the beauty of New Orleans, Maria was most impressed with the sadness of its slave market. There men, women, and children, neatly dressed, were seated on long benches. One girl, Maria noticed, was whiter than she was herself. A bright-looking child Maria questioned said that the girl had been bought by a trader in Kentucky and was brought from there to New Orleans. How silly I am to be homesick, she thought, when this poor child will never see her home again! It was good that no buyers came in. Maria could not bear to talk to the trader. She felt nauseated. People were for sale there like toys. When she came out in the fresh air, she realized that she had been feeling a little sick all the time.

Later she visited a Negro church and was impressed by

the sadness in the slaves' voices. On plantations, Maria was treated more courteously than on some trains in the North. Everywhere, though, she heard discussions of slavery. She could not accept the idea that such an institution could exist in a free country.

Their tour took them up the Alabama River to Mobile, then by stagecoach to Savannah, Georgia, and by steamer to Charleston. Maria was entertained in all those cities. In Nashville, Tennessee, she enjoyed meeting the widow of President James Polk, a well-read woman from New England.

In May, Maria bade Prue good-by, looking forward with real anticipation to their trip abroad.

Back home in Nantucket, she could not help contrasting the strong-minded women of New England with the southern women she had met. Her sister Kate was getting ready for her marriage to Owen Dame. The severe discipline of Orthodox Quakerism would be hard for her sister, Maria suspected.

She was happy about an article in Emerson's *The United States Magazine* about funds being raised by the women of Boston to give her a larger revolving telescope. The project had been organized by Elizabeth Peabody, who was considered "the most learned woman" by Boston intellectuals. A little observatory was to be included in the three-thousand-dollar project. Emerson also officially announced that Maria was going abroad to help the cause of science by intelligent study and observation. Maria smiled as she made preparations for the dream trip.

In the latter part of June, Maria went to New York and embarked with Prue on the steamship *Arabia*. In her big purse she carried letters of introduction to great scientists, astronomers, and mathematicians, but she was also eager to see London, Paris, and Rome. As the skyline of brownstone and grayish houses accented by the pointed spire of Trinity Church receded, she did not feel homesick, although the harbor bells of Nantucket seemed far away already.

For the next few days they lived in a hazy world, for the ship was enveloped in fog. The horn kept blowing like a lost phantom, but Maria was undaunted. She and Prue spent their time eating, sleeping, and getting acquainted with the few passengers on deck. They went to the bow of the ship and saw the phosphorous in the wake shining like stars in the ocean.

After ten days, a sailor called, "Land!" and the passengers rushed to the rail. Maria realized that she would be glad to step on solid ground again. In a special large wallet, she placed her letter from Edward Everett, president of Harvard. There were introductions from Dr. Bond and his son, as well as from other scientists in America. She also had the first photograph ever made of a star, which George had sent to her along with his letter about the great possibilities of photography as an aid to the study of astronomy.

While in Liverpool, Maria visited the famous observatory there and its director, John Hartnup. Nathaniel Hawthorne, the novelist, was American consul in that seaport, but Maria was afraid he would not call after she sent her letter of introduction, because he was said to be very shy.

When Hawthorne arrived, he did not say much. Maria thought that he looked like his pictures. His hair stuck out on both sides and she had an impulse to smooth it. Hawthorne seemed willing to help her in any way he could during her stay abroad.

She was invited to the home of the founder of the Liverpool Observatory, John Taylor, an astronomer as well as a wealthy cotton merchant.

She enjoyed it all, but she was glad to reach London

and settle down on Cork Street. The parlor there had too much furniture, including a piano, a sideboard, a sofa and an easy chair, many oil paintings and waxed flowers. Maria was determined to see first the homes and work places of Sir Isaac Newton, the scientist, and of Samuel Johnson, famous for his dictionary.

Learning from the guidebook that Sir Isaac Newton had lived in the St. Martin's section of London, Maria arranged for a cab driver to take them there the next day. Prue had stayed overnight with Maria and was now going to her aunt's home in a different section of London. A note from the aunt said that a servant would bring the family carriage that evening.

"Newton will be first tomorrow," said Maria. "Sir Isaac Newton discovered the principle of gravity."

"I always thought that Newton, or Sir Isaac, I should say, sounded stuffy," Prue offered. "Just sitting around and letting apples fall and getting so much praise."

"But he did more than that," Maria said. "He was always inquiring the reason why."

"Maybe I could imagine him better if you have some pictures in that guidebook."

Maria turned over the pages and handed the book to Prue.

"This one with a wig, taken when he was a student, looks rather wild," the girl said hopefully.

"I think he was the greatest scientist of the eighteenth century," said Maria. She picked up her little Dolland telescope from the table and let Prue look through it. "His telescope is an eight-inch and mine is ten. That is the diameter of the main mirror."

"I know that the diameter is a line through the center of the object. Daddy taught me some plane geometry. Diameter can mean the thickness."

Maria was glad that Prue had tutored with her father and knew something more than needlework and playing "The Maiden's Prayer."

"Well, 'Eight inches was the diameter of his main mirror,' " she read from the book. "The tube was almost six feet. The so-called Newtonian reflector gathers light by means of a curved mirror at the bottom end of the tube. The curve of the mirror directs the light rays to a second mirror. An eyepiece at the side of the tube brings the rays to a focus and magnifies the image they form just as you've seen it through my little Dolland."

At that point the Swift servant arrived, and Maria was rather glad to see Prue depart. I'll have to slow down my explanations, she resolved.

The next morning they drove to the Newton Hotel. "It could be any old inn in London," was Prue's comment, and even Maria was a little nonplussed. There was not even a little observatory like theirs on top of the bank. Maria suggested going in a nearby door to get more information. She saw a barmaid pouring drinks. "Where did Sir Isaac Newton live?" she asked.

Going to a door, the girl pointed to a house by the church and said, "He studied up there." Maria saw a little oblong observatory made of wood and blackened by soot.

Prue's face was blank.

"What do you think of it?" Maria asked.

"He must have gotten dirty up there, and his hair must have blown a lot, and he never saw the apple fall around here."

At least she was putting herself in Newton's place and seeing him as a real person, not a stuffed owl. Maria reflected, If I ever teach again, I must make things real.

When they were eating in the dining room, Prue said,

[87]

"I think he must have been at his mother's house in the country when he saw the apple and got ideas about gravity."

"He didn't jump to the idea of gravity all at once," Maria replied. "Although he looked wild, he was cautious about giving out a definite statement. He figured out the motion of the moon around the earth. If she followed the earth, she had to be attracted. The moon is falling in the earth's direction, but is going so fast that she misses it. She continued going because the earth is round. Newton realized that the path of the apple and the curved orbit of the moon were both round and dependent on the same cause. That was the way he got the idea of gravity."

"I wish we could see his house and the apple tree," Prue said earnestly. The exchange had prompted the most interest Prue had shown, except for her attraction to the hair styles from Paris and a mild leaning toward opera. Maria decided to write the occupants of Newton's house at Woolsthorpe Manor.

"Now, on to Dr. Johnson!" said Prue cheerily.

On Fleet Street, Maria and Prue walked through narrow passages to the room where Samuel Johnson wrote his dictionary. Prue liked Samuel Johnson as a person and she did not mind going through gloomy halls to the room where he worked. "My father has his dictionary," she said proudly. "But I like our Noah Webster's better. It isn't so hard.

"Boswell must have had fun writing about Samuel," she went on cheerfully. "I wonder why they didn't live someplace like Newton's house in the country?"

"I suppose he wanted to meet his congenial friends," Maria said. "You know, Edgar Allan Poe was in Boston, and he said that when he lived in the outskirts of New

York at Fordham he rowed to New York to meet writer friends and editors."

"He must have been tired after going by boat," Prue commented. "I wonder if he read his poem 'The Bells' for them to praise."

"Criticize," corrected Maria, glad to see that Prue was thinking of Johnson and Poe as writers like those living in her day.

"I think Dr. Johnson was dictatorial," Maria said. "He wouldn't have liked criticism."

"I don't know that word, but I know Johnson was bossy."

"Yes, indeed," said Maria. "But he was a scholar."

Later they went to the House of Commons, where Maria enjoyed the fiery debate on the mutiny of Indian soldiers. Prue was more interested in going to the opera. Unfortunately, since Maria was tone-deaf, she could not enjoy the music.

Prue also enjoyed the dances and the young people at her aunt's home. Both of them enjoyed the theater. Maria had received invitations to homes of scientists outside of London. Prue stayed at her aunt's house while Maria went to visit Admiral William H. Smyth, an astronomer at Greenwich Observatory.

The two-hour trip to Aylesbury by railroad through flowering gardens and the stagecoach ride to Smyth's home in the village of Stone were not wearisome. Maria was happy to meet the scientist. He had favored her receiving the king's medal as first discoverer of the comet, and he was the author of her favorite book, *Double Stars*. His wife, also an astronomer, had written to reserve a seat for Maria inside the coach, but it was crowded and Maria was obliged to climb a ladder to reach the topside. At first she was frightened, but the weather was so delightful that she forgot the danger and enjoyed the drive. Admiral Smyth had photographed the moon and was greatly interested in George Bond's pictures of the stars.

Maria also enjoyed meeting Dr. Neil Arnott, the author of the first physics book she had ever studied. He told her that he had started the book on shipboard after he had studied the stars on a long, stormy voyage.

Two of the high points in her trip were a visit to the Royal Observatory on the Thames River and her stay in the home of Sir George Airy and his wife. Sir George was the astronomer royal and headed the observatory at Greenwich. She had heard that he was called the Bear of Blackheath, but to her he was a delightful companion who had confirmed her discovery of the comet. She later found out that George Bond had written him that she ranked among America's finest astronomers. That night she would go to bed happy with the assurance of George's continued interest.

Through Mrs. Airy she was invited to the home of Dr. William Whewell, the master of Trinity College, Cambridge University. He disagreed with Maria on everything from Emerson to Elizabeth Browning—as Mrs. Airy said, they "riled each other." But Maria did enjoy visiting the lodgings of the Airys' sons and seeing the life of Cambridge with its ancient customs.

9

Alone on the Continent

Maria looked forward to visiting the home of Sir John Herschel at Collingwood. She sent her letter of introduction with high hopes but did not immediately receive her invitation to come.

"I wish I could go," Prue said, "but anyway, I think the Newton house in the country will answer your inquiry."

"The present occupants may not like to have visitors," Maria warned. Then the Swifts' servant appeared, and Prue was off to the Tower of London.

Maria was just as glad that Prue wasn't going to Collingwood, since there was no time to answer if she followed Sir John's schedule.

She got out her books to be sure of Sir John's background, but she knew it by heart from her father's talking about the Herschels when they were searching the skies in the little observatory at the bank. She wanted to make it interesting for Prue. It will really be a test of my teaching if Prue wants us to stay abroad longer than we planned, she reasoned.

The story of William Herschel, the father of Sir John, was almost a rags-to-riches saga. William had been a young German musician in an orchestra in Bath, England. He was an amateur astronomer and had aroused the interest of scientists in England by discovering the planet Uranus in 1781, two years before the treaty ending the American Revolution.

Mr. Mitchell's letter said to tell Sir John that their cousin Benjamin Franklin had written to Sir William Herschel congratulating him on the discovery of the planet. "You would have gotten results sooner in America, because the weather was better and there were more clear nights for observation," Franklin had written. Maria was a little doubtful about the tactfulness of bringing up the weather's being better in America. It seemed advisable to wait and see whether Sir John was really the Bear of Collingwood.

She liked his comfortable red-brick house, on spacious grounds near a lake. In his library he welcomed her beside a small hearth fire. Although he had not received her letter of introduction, he said, "My dear, I know you through letters from your father."

Maria thought that he looked like Dr. Bond, somewhat stooped and with ruffled white hair. When they were seated by the glowing fire, he told her of his childhood when his father was the astronomer royal and the time when his Aunt Caroline was his confidante and companion while she was an assistant in the Royal Observatory. She had been glad to escape a German mother who had wanted her to be a housekeeper, not an astronomer.

Maria remembered that Miss Herschel had discovered several comets and helped with her brother's work on nebulae. "Your Aunt Caroline was the first woman astronomer in the Royal Observatory in England, I think," said Maria.

"Yes, though German-born and tutored there," Sir John added. He went to his desk and drew out some sheets of manuscript. "I will give you a sheet of foolscap from one of her articles with her autograph, for you are

[92]

the first woman American astronomer."

Maria felt comforted that someone understood her lonely place in American life. She folded the paper carefully, for Miss Herschel's hand had touched it.

"And then," the gentle voice went on, "my aunt returned to Germany. It is like renewing my relationship with her to talk to you, another woman astronomer." Maria met his kind eyes with understanding.

That night she talked with Sir John's wife and children, and he told her of his famous expedition to explore the stars in the southern part of the world. Sir William and Sir John had also swept with their telescopes the northern skies from Slough, in England.

"You must be the only man who ever observed the whole star sphere, including the cape of Africa," Maria said. She was surprised that he had stayed so long over there. But then, remembering all that he had observed, she thought she must make it clear to Prue later.

At the dinner table, Sir John indulged in nonsense rhymes, and the children joined in. Maria enjoyed herself, but she kept wishing that she could talk to Sir John sometime again as they had in the library.

Her wish was fulfilled the next morning, when Sir John toured the grounds with her. His white hair was blowing wildly, and she was reminded of his portrait. They visited the barn, and Maria was shocked to see the telescope that Sir John had used at the Cape of Good Hope dismantled and in many pieces. He talked to her of his work in other lines of science. His articles were on optics, chemistry, and double stars, as well as photographic processes.

"You have done so much in other fields . . . ," but Maria could not take her eyes away from the old telescope. "The glass is intact," she said. "You should put the telescope in a museum."

[93]

Sir John looked as embarrassed as a small boy. "What would your Aunt Caroline think?" Maria insisted.

He laughed. "You sound like her," he said ruefully. "I must be more like Newton in adhering to one line of science until I finish one phase. It is true I should assemble this instrument and put it in a museum.

"I shall say good-by to you now. . . ." He kissed her on the forehead. Maria felt as if she had known him always.

They returned to the house, and Maria bade Mrs. Herschel and the children good-by. On her way back to London, Maria found that she was thinking of Sir John as one of her warmest friends. She hoped that she could convey her impressions to Prue.

However, there was no time to talk to the girl about Collingwood before they left on a scheduled trip to the Lake Country with a party of young people.

The peace and quiet of Wordsworth's country reminded Maria of the Hudson River Highland at home. She and Prue met Kate Southey, the daughter of the poet laureate. Kate had many American friends and wished to visit the United States. Prue was amused to learn that in addition to his poetry Robert Southey had written the original version of the children's story "The Three Bears."

Although Maria spent a good deal of time in observatories in Scotland, and in visiting cathedrals and churches, she managed to squeeze in sightseeing trips to the Shakespeare country too.

On their return to London in the fall of 1857, they found a pile of mail from home. Prue came in waving a letter. "A nice, long letter from Daddy," she said. Then her face changed as she turned the page and she looked down to the end.

"Bad news!" she called out. She began to cry. Maria

[94]

put her arms around the girl and patted her shoulder. When Prue stopped sobbing, she said, "It's really bad news. Read it!"

Maria saw the usually careful penmanship straggling across the page in a manner not at all like the precise banker's style. Prue's father must be upset and worried. "Wall Street's gone mad," she read. "We're penniless. You must come home. I've ordered a draft deposited to your account in London for your return passage. Tell Miss Mitchell."

"He isn't exactly penniless," Prue said. "Anyway, I'm going home to the boy he didn't like." Her face lighted up, and she began to wipe away her tears. "I did want to see Mr. Newton's house, because this British boy from Oxford lived near there, but he was rather stuffy. Oh me, oh my, won't Percy be surprised! He thought I was a rich American." She began to trill the old song, " 'We'll pipe and we'll sing, love,/We'll dance in a ring, love.' "

Maria heard the girl's lilting voice as if from a distance. How quickly her mood had changed. General Swift had lost so much money that they had to return to the United States. . . . The words went around and around in her mind.

After she had comforted Prue about missing Paris and all the styles, Maria went to her room and paced up and down as she had used to do on the beach at Nantucket. At last, toward morning, she made up her mind not to go home until she had seen Rome, where Galileo had studied the stars and suffered in the Inquisition. Instead of this crowded room, she would find a lower-priced place where she could live on her computing salary. Being alone in strange places, she would miss Prue. She wished she were going home to George, but that could never be. . . .

Prue wrote her a few letters after arriving home. Her

[95]

father had agreed to her marrying her American. Somehow Maria felt that knowing Prue had helped her to understand a certain type of American girl. Perhaps she could teach, later on. Now, she spent several days searching hopelessly for another place to live.

Up and down dirty, dark stairs Maria searched, and she finally found an attic with a small window. As she worked away at her computing for the *Harvard Almanac*, she realized that she could not go to Paris until she received her check from Commander Davis. When General Swift had paid the cost of living, she had not noticed the price of hansom cabs.

Having heard Sir George Airy discuss the work of his protégé Professor John Couch Adams in discovering the planet Neptune, Maria wanted to read accounts in the French publications to learn why Urbain Leverrier had received so much of the credit. Since Leverrier was now head of the Paris Observatory and Sir George Airy had given her a letter of introduction, she felt that in fairness to both men she needed to know both sides.

Walking to the British Museum, where files of French newspapers were available, was not too difficult. Fortunately, reading French was no problem, either, though she shivered at the thought of speaking the language.

The English newspapers upheld Sir George Airy's claim that Adams, an honor student, had written him in 1845 about the location of the planet. He reported that a new planet could be looked for beyond Sir William Herschel's Uranus. Adams' calculations indicated the location of Uranus and the longitude and latitude of the new planet.

Maria knew that from the time of the discovery of Uranus by Sir William Herschel astronomers had reported slight deviations in the planet's movements. Granting that the law of gravity held, there must be some force acting on Uranus besides the known factors. Could it be another planet? Most of those trying to solve the problem were stopped by the difficult calculations.

Although Adams had passed mathematical honors examinations, Sir George doubted that a student would be capable of solving the problem of the strange movements of Uranus. Airy decided to test Adams with certain questions developed from Airy's own observations about the error in the radius vector of Uranus, its distance from the sun. With his mathematical background and knowledge about the planet, Adams could have answered the questions, but he probably was not very confident about his prediction and did not answer. Sir George was busy and did not follow up the Adams correspondence.

In the meantime a young Frenchman, Urbain Leverrier, from the province of Normandy in France, had become a professor of astronomy at the Polytechnical School, which had recently been founded by Napoleon III. The famous mathematician Arago suggested to Leverrier that the movements of Uranus would be an interesting subject for study.

Leverrier first took up the movements of Jupiter and Saturn to see if they might have affected Uranus, but none of the perturbations was sufficiently large to explain the strange movements of Uranus.

He believed that there was some continuous reason— perhaps an unknown planet. Could there be one inside the orbit of Uranus? Not likely, for in that case Jupiter and Saturn would be affected, but they were not.

He tried to rule out the deviations caused by Jupiter and Saturn and other known causes and then to locate the place of an outer planet able to affect Uranus. This was difficult, for there was nothing known about the elusive body except the microscopic perturbations it caused in Uranus a thousand million miles away.

In June 1846, when Leverrier announced to the world his problematical position for the planet, Professor Airy was shocked to find that Leverrier's position for the new planet was within one degree of the place Adams had assigned to it.

Professor Airy propounded for Leverrier the same question he had submitted to Adams. Could the new observations explain the errors of the radius vector (distance from the sun)?

Leverrier answered, explaining the errors, and the existence of a new planet was officially recognized. The British astronomer royal wrote to Professor James Challis at Cambridge Observatory to institute a search for the new planet, since the telescope there was larger than the ones available to him.

Professor Challis actually had seen the new planet twice without realizing it, for he lacked a map containing telescopic stars down to the tenth magnitude, which he could then have compared with his own observations. Such a map had been completed in Germany, in certain sections, but was not available in Great Britain.

At the same time, Adams wrote Sir George Airy, making additions to his information. He also answered the question about the radius vector.

The British Association met that year at Southampton, and Sir John Herschel was one of its divisional presidents. In his address on September 10, 1846, he said of the researches of Leverrier and Adams, "The last year has given to us the new minor planet Astraca; it has done more—it has given us the probable prospect of another. We see it as Columbus saw America from the shores of Spain. Its movements have been felt trembling along the far-reaching line of our analysis with a certainty hardly inferior to ocular demonstration."

Maria could imagine how his deep voice had stirred

the audience, but the credit for discovering the comet was still hovering between England and France.

Meanwhile, Leverrier wrote to Dr. Johann Gottfried Galle, head of the observatory at Berlin, reporting that the new planet was now close to a certain position and that he could know it was not a star because it was a disk and not a point. Dr. Galle got the letter on September 23, 1846, and that night he saw a star that did seem to be a disk. He compared Bremiker's uncompleted star chart in the section just completed and there was no such star. It must be the planet.

By October 1, 1846, Adams heard the news at Cambridge and realized that England was out of the running. Sir George Airy thought that Adams should have recognition for his research, but Leverrier's papers had been published and the French were annoyed when a claim was set up for Adams to share in the discovery.

Maria knew that Adams was not resentful at losing a share in the final acclaim. Nevertheless, Airy and other British astronomers did fight for Adams to be given a part of the credit for the discovery of Neptune. The bitterness had continued for over ten years.

Sir George having been the leader of the pro-Adams group, Maria feared that his letter of introduction would be received coldly in Paris, since Leverrier was now the head of the Paris Observatory. Her trip to Paris was marred by her worries about her reception there.

She arrived on a dark and rainy day and found a reasonably priced pension, although it was some distance from the observatory.

Leverrier did go through the courteous motions of calling on her and entertaining her. December 15 was the day set for her to see the observatory, but it turned out to provide just another social gathering at which only the lady guests spoke to Maria. At ten o'clock, Leverrier showed her the downstairs rooms of the observatory but not the domes, for he made it clear that he did not expect her to understand an observatory. She was not invited to the Academy of Science, where the French scientist Louis Pasteur was presenting accounts of his famous experiments with preservation of food.

Maria was bitterly disappointed not to have seen the observatory, but she did attend lectures at the Sorbonne.

Finally, she decided to go on to Rome. After all, Galileo was one of her greatest heroes. She wrote a letter asking if she could accompany Nathaniel Hawthorne's party.

He invited her to meet him and make arrangements. Later, he wrote in his diary: "This morning, Miss Mitchell, the celebrated lady of Nantucket, called. She had brought a letter of introduction to me while consul, and her business now was to see if we could take her as one of our party to Rome whither she likewise is bound. We readily consented, for she seems to be a simple, strong, healthy-humored woman, who will not fling herself as a burden on our shoulders; my only wonder is that a person evidently so able to take care of herself should come about having an escort."

10

No Women Allowed?

Maria and the Hawthornes journeyed to Marseilles on a tugboat, then overland by stage through mountain passes where robbers were said to lurk. Maria liked the quiet Hawthorne, with his faraway eyes, and admired his gentle wife, but she loved their little son, Julian. Maria had put her money in her stocking and refused to entertain the idea of robbers searching for it, but she held the little boy's hand anyway, during that part of the ride. Then she tried to remember all that she knew of Galileo in Rome.

In the gray winter twilight, as they entered Rome, she was thinking of Galileo and his trial by the Inquisition. He had rejected the view of the Catholic Church that Copernicus was wrong. She could not read Italian, but she would find references in Latin books. She might write an article, she thought, or use the material she found in talks to women, if colleges were opened to them.

When she was settled in the city near the Hawthornes, she began to study all the books she could find about Galileo. She knew his belief in the theory of Copernicus that the earth rotated around the sun had caused him to be summoned before the Inquisition.

In a Latin book, she learned that Galileo was born at Pisa in 1564. At seventeen, he was sent to the University of Pisa to study medicine, but he preferred to read Euclid and Archimedes. Then he decided he wanted to be not a doctor but a mathematician. At twenty-six, he was appointed lecturer in mathematics at the university. Then he became interested in the writings of Giordano Bruno and believed in the Copernican theory. He also challenged the scholars who believed in Aristotle's idea of falling bodies, and this made him unpopular. He joined the teaching force of the University of Padua, as professor of mathematics in the Republic of Venice.

The Venetians probably hired him because of his practical inventions, first a thermometer and then something like a modern slide rule. But more significant to Maria was his invention of the telescope in 1609.

Some spectacle makers from Flanders had invented a form of spyglass, about the strength of an opera glass, with a magnification value of about three. Galileo grasped the idea in one night and increased the magnifying power up to 8 or 10 percent, and he called the result a telescope.

He took the Venetian senate up to the top of the Campanile to show off his invention. From there, a ship could not only be seen but could be recognized fifty miles away. Galileo's first book, *The Starry Messenger,* told of turning the telescope on the moon and four planets, satellites of Jupiter.

The news of the satellites made Galileo famous, but also upheld the theory of Copernicus, which was opposed to the ideas of the established church. Certain propositions were held to be true: first, that the sun was immovable, at the center of the heavens; second, that the earth was not at the center of the heavens and was not immovable but moved in a double motion.

In 1610, Galileo showed with his telescope that the satellites of Jupiter were rotating around her. He also proved that Venus progressed from full circle to a crescent. This discovery caused his expulsion from Padua.

Then Cosimo de Medici invited him to become philosopher to the Grand Ducal Court of Tuscany. There Galileo discovered many new stars and nebulae, saw what appeared to be a triple form of Saturn, and observed sunspots. That the sun could be imperfect was a most irritating idea to theologians.

Galileo made the mistake of going to Rome in 1616 to persuade his friends not to prohibit the teaching of Copernicus' theories, which had been proven by the recent astronomical studies with the telescope. The church formally forbade his teaching the Copernican theory. He hoped to see a more intellectual pope elected.

On the accession of Pope Urban VIII in 1623, Galileo was well received, but his book entitled *Dialogue on the Great World Systems, Ptolemaic and Copernican* caused an uproar. He believed that the same physical forces operated throughout the universe. By turning his telescope on the moon and Jupiter, he put an end to the classical belief that the heavens were perfect and unchanging.

One of the characters in his *Dialogue* was named Simplicius. Urban believed that Galileo intended that stupid character to represent the pope. People got the impression that Simplicius really spoke the pope's ideas. This was an insult.

Galileo was called to Rome on April 12, 1633. There were ten judges on the Inquisition, seven favorable to the pope. Galileo was interrogated about his purpose in writing the book. The Inquisition claimed that there was a document prohibiting Galileo's teaching the theory of Copernicus in any way whatsoever, including the writing of books.

During the time of the trial, he was taken into another room where he was shown the instruments of torture, as if they were about to be used. Having studied medicine,

Galileo knew the terrible pain the rack could cause. There were people living in Rome who remembered the burning of Giordano Bruno at the stake for declaring his belief in the Copernican theory.

Maria could imagine it all and knew how much it must have hurt Galileo to recant his belief after seeing proofs of it in the heavens. The petty restrictions of his later life, when he was ill and blind, were unpleasant but could not equal the despair he must have known in publicly denying his belief. She felt that she was on sacred ground when she walked near the place where he had suffered.

Those first four days in Rome were more precious to Maria than all the other days of her travels. She went alone to St. Peter's and the Vatican, to the Roman Forum and on to the Colosseum, where she walked around the whole circumference. She could not believe that she was actually standing among the ruins and not dreaming. Later, the Hawthornes called, and she took Mrs. Hawthorne to the same spot.

Maria had written to Father Angelo de Secchi asking to see the observatory of the Collegio Romano. The priest, who had lectured in the United States, was a progressive astronomer and was now director of the observatory. After several days, she returned from a drive and met two priests descending a flight of stairs in the house where she was staying. The older one asked, "Are you Miss Mitchell?" He was Father de Secchi, and accompanying him was a young attendant.

They went with her into her apartment, and Father de Secchi showed her photo negatives of Saturn. She hoped that they could forget the criticism of Galileo for studying Saturn and proving the planet to be triple. Galileo had gone through a period of doubt when the two attendant rings had disappeared but kept up his courage, believing that they would reappear, as they did. They had seemed to disappear because they were so thin when seen on edge. Now Maria could tell George about Father de Secchi's photographing of Saturn.

She wanted to see the observatory of the Collegio Romano, which was in the monastery behind the Church of St. Ignacio. Father de Secchi was its director.

After a time she asked Father de Secchi if she might visit his observatory, but she saw by his face that she had made a mistake.

He said that he had already asked his superiors, and only a cardinal could give her permission, because the observatory, being on church property, was part of the monastery. Women were not allowed there. He told her that she could take her request to Cardinal Antonelli himself. After a fortnight she received a permit through a young Italian, the nephew of a monsignor. It was written on parchment and signed by Cardinal Antonelli.

Maria also erred in thinking that she could bring a woman interpreter. Father de Secchi said that she could meet him at the Church of St. Ignacio an hour and a half before Ave Maria vespers or at sunset. He would conduct her through the church into the observatory, but her woman interpreter must stop in the church.

The woman begged to go into the observatory so that she could help Maria with her Italian, but Father de Secchi insisted that she go no farther, because the holy father had given admission to only one person.

Maria and her guide worked their way through long halls and winding stairs of the monastery and through the astronomical library, where young astronomers worked, and at last Maria reached the dome and the telescope. It was nearly the size of the twelve-inch one in Washington. The dome was built on old Roman foundations, and Father de Secchi was now able to give out reports of the stars in the city where Galileo had been tried for believing that the earth moved around the sun and had been compelled to renounce his beliefs.

Maria wanted to stay until dark to study the stars from the observatory, but Father de Secchi told her that permission did not extend beyond nightfall. She felt more like Cinderella than a scientist as she hurried homeward alone.

In Florence, Maria visited Mary Somerville, who had interpreted in English the works of the great French scientist Laplace and who was a famous mathematician in her own right. Maria found her pleasantly chatty about everything from the Gold Rush in California to the tails of comets. She was interested in George Bond's photograph of the double star, which Maria had presented to the observatory, and asked about the Bonds and other American scientists.

The mathematician spoke with a strong Scottish accent, being a member of the Fairfax family related to George Washington through his half brother Lawrence's marriage to Ann Fairfax. She told Maria, "When Lieutenant Fairfax was ordered to America, Washington wrote to him as a family relative and asked him to make him a visit. Lieutenant Fairfax applied to his commanding officer for permission to accept and it was refused. They never met, and much to the regret of the Fairfax family the letter from Washington was lost. The Fairfaxes of Virginia are of the same family, and occasionally some member of the American branch returns to see his Scottish cousins."

Mrs. Somerville's comments on letters from the son of Professor Nathaniel Bowditch showed her friendliness to Americans. At the age of seventy-seven, she was alert and interested in every improvement, hopeful, cheery, and happy.

Maria had been in Europe over a year when she visited

Alexander von Humboldt in Berlin. His servant showed her into an anteroom hung with deer horns and carpeted with tiger skins. When Humboldt entered, he bowed in a courtly manner. He talked about Thomas Jefferson, with whom he had stayed most of his three months in the United States. He also knew Dr. Alexander Bache, Sir George Airy, and Lieutenant Matthew F. Maury of the Washington Observatory. He was familiar with President Buchanan's administration and felt sure that Kansas would not become a slave state.

At the age of eighty-nine, Humboldt was preparing his fifth volume of *Kosmos*. Maria was sure no young science student ever left his presence uncheered.

After visiting other German astronomers, Maria returned to England. There she heard Charles Dickens read *The Cricket on the Hearth* and was thrilled with Charles Kean's performance in *King Lear*. A few days later, she sailed for home.

When she arrived back in the United States, Maria learned that the campaign she had heard of in Boston to raise money to give her a telescope had become a project of the women of America. Elizabeth Peabody of Boston and Mrs. Joseph Willard originated the idea of presenting a gift to the first American woman scientist. The telescope lens was larger than Maria's own little Dolland and would help her to widen her field of investigation.

She left New York with happy thoughts for the future, and her father met her at the ferry dock in Nantucket. At home, Sally shook her head when they entered the bedroom. Maria's mother looked at her with unseeing eyes. She had recognized no one while her daughter was in Europe. Maria was glad that she did not need to regret having gone.

Soon her mother was able to walk about the house and needed to be watched. Maria did not often go to Boston with her father. He was now a member of the Visiting Committee of Harvard College. He often saw George Bond, who had become director of the Harvard Observatory in 1859 after the death of his father. It was a sad year for George, because both his wife and his youngest child had died of tuberculosis. Maria wrote a letter of sympathy and he replied, telling about his work on drawings and measurements of Saturn. He left out his little jokes at first and Maria wrote impersonally, but their correspondence was a comfort.

Maria's mother talked of the past and thought all the children were at home. Maria could not leave her for long. Phebe and Kate were married and had left Nantucket, but Sally and Ann were still living on the island. Andrew and Henry were studying tides and currents in New York, and Forster was superintendent of Haverford College, in Pennsylvania. Mrs. Mitchell sometimes called Francis, who worked in the cashier's cage in the bank downstairs, by the names of her other sons.

George wrote Maria about his observations on Donati's comet, and with her new gift telescope she located it independently. She set up a little observatory of her own behind the Coffin School. There she enjoyed reading George's articles about Comet II and prepared for publication articles of her own about locating double stars and the eclipse of 1861.

Her mother died that year, and Maria and her father found the rooms over the bank lonely, so they bought a small house in Lynn, Massachusetts, where Kate and her husband, Owen Dame, were living. William Mitchell had sold the little Nantucket farm and given up his work as cashier in the bank, so with Maria's savings they were able to live. Maria was still earning a salary computing for the *Harvard Almanac.* With the little observatory next to the house, her life centered around the study of the stars.

Life was happy, but sometimes she felt the need for more exciting accomplishments.

One day in August of 1862, a letter came from Rufus Babcock, trustee of the college for women newly founded by Matthew Vassar at Poughkeepsie, New York. Maria had followed with interest articles about higher education for women. Mr. Babcock asked for a personal interview with her. He said that Mr. Vassar was interested in her teaching astronomy and heading an observatory at Vassar.

Maria could hardly believe the words on the paper as she read them aloud to her father. She knew that people argued bitterly about education for women. Many believed that girls would become ill if they studied too hard. Others joked, saying, nonsense, women needed only to know how to sew, do housework, play a little on the piano, and dabble at china painting. They called Matthew Vassar an old fool whose college would turn girls away from being good housewives. They were sure Vassar's idea was just a wild scheme of a rich old man.

But Maria's father thought that the offer presented a wonderful opportunity to tell others about the stars. Besides, Maria would have the honor of being the first woman to bring science to the Vassar girls. According to the letter, Mr. Vassar believed that she had shown some interest in education for women and might cooperate in making the college a "magnificent experiment."

But I don't know enough, she thought. I've never been to college myself. My father and Cyrus Peirce were my only teachers. Professor Peirce, though, had been appointed head of the first normal school in America. Maria's father sensed her feelings but suggested that she answer the letter at once and invite Mr. Babcock to dinner.

Another angle intruded. If Maria was given the job,

what would her father do, alone in their little home? He was getting older, and he had been with her longer than with his other children. He could go to visit John Greenleaf Whittier in the poet's cottage on the shores of the Merrimack River, but that was a very special jaunt, not a continuing arrangement.

To keep from worrying, Maria began to make a list of all that she would need for a good New England dinner. She would do it herself with the help of a girl from Nantucket.

Mr. Babcock accepted the invitation, but on the appointed day the kitchen helper was unable to come, so Maria prepared and served the meal to the fastidious guest by herself. Then, in the little observatory at the end of the garden, she handled her well-adjusted telescope. Mr. Babcock wrote Matthew Vassar, sent along recommendations from Salem Normal School, Harvard College, and Brown University, and invited Maria's father to come and live with her at Vassar.

Maria would have an apartment of her own in the new building with its observatory. She was offered a tentative salary of fifteen hundred dollars, which she considered too large an amount because of her lack of higher education. The offer had to be agreed upon by the president of Vassar, Milo P. Jewett, who was away at that time.

Maria was happy that her father could come with her and overjoyed to receive a letter of congratulation from Mr. Vassar. He later wrote that the walls of the college now had a roof and there was hope that the buildings would be completed by 1864. He regretted that the Civil War was obstructing the building process.

Women left their homes to nurse soldiers, join societies to aid the war effort, distribute supplies, and raise money. Many of them, Maria thought, would not be content to return to their former idle and restricted lives.

Nevertheless, debating continued in the press about higher education for women. Milo P. Jewett, Vassar's president, and some of the board were opposed to women as professors, but Matthew Vassar and Benson Lossing, the historian and teacher, were firm about having Maria as a professor of astronomy.

She began to think that the war would never end and the buildings at Vassar would never be finished. Because of her Quaker background she was opposed to war. However, her brother Andrew, who had been close to death in the Navy, was now captain of a merchant ship under Admiral Farragut in Mobile Bay. William Forster was teaching emancipated slaves near Nashville, Tennessee.

Through Mrs. Sarah Josepha Hale, editor of *Godey's Lady's Book,* Maria heard that Mr. Vassar had bought a twelve-inch achromatic telescope. Achromatic meant that things seen through the telescope would have images without colors caused by prism effects.

The war's end brought Maria happiness in many ways, but the president of Vassar indicated that he was opposed to a woman's being on the college staff for such a high salary. Later he offered Maria the jobs of astronomy teacher and head of the observatory at a salary of eight hundred dollars a year, with board for her and her father. She decided to accept and arranged for the two of them to take a trip by boat up the Hudson River to Poughkeepsie to see the college and the apartment where they would live.

The voyage reminded Maria of her trip with her sister Ann to Chestnut Ridge, Dutchess County, when they were girls. They had landed at the dock in Poughkeepsie, where some Nantucket trading ships were anchored. She had enjoyed the town then, and now looked forward to revisiting the place where her Quaker ancestors had fled

[111]

for refuge during the American Revolution. Some of her Mitchell and Coleman relatives still lived there. She felt as though she was coming home and a new life was beginning. She would write George and tell him the good news.

A week later, the Boston newspaper carried the headline "George Bond, Director of Harvard Observatory, Dies." Maria dropped the paper from her hands. She could not bear to see more.

Later, she read on about the gold medal awarded to George by the Royal Astronomical Society in London for outstanding work on the Donati comet of 1858. George had detected eleven other comets. Mention was made of his application of photography to astronomical observation.

The medal had probably come too late, for George had died in February. Tears came into Maria's eyes and coursed down her cheeks.

Her father came in and put his arm around her. "This is hard, very hard," he said. "But thee must put thy heart into this new work at Vassar." Maria pressed his hand and nodded her acceptance of what he said, but she kept thinking of George as he used to be.

11

Underpaid Distinction

Maria and her father took a hansom cab to "Vassar's Folly," as the college was nicknamed by opponents of the college for women. By the gateway was a small porter's lodge, where visitors asked permission to enter. The gatekeeper bowed deeply, and Maria was reminded of the entrance to castles in England. Behind a low stone wall, she saw a building like the Tuileries in France, and above its door were the words "Vassar Female College." There was a long driveway.

In the distance, beyond the college building, was the round dome of the observatory, looking like a smaller castle, with a circular drive in front. It stood on a rocky knoll at the eastern edge of the huge campus, high above the Hudson River.

As they came nearer, the cryptlike entrance to the observatory reminded Maria of the door of a wizard's house. From the first floor they climbed a narrow, winding iron stairway to the room where there was an astronomical clock connected with a brass chronometer for recording observations. This was the Mitchells' sitting room. The windows and walls were not decorated, and the plain chairs were placed parallel to the walls as Maria always wished them to be. When Sally came from Nantucket for a visit, she would probably set about adjusting them, Maria thought, as she had done in the gray-shingled house on Vestal Street.

Maria felt no twinge of homesickness. Only Sally and Ann were still living on the island, but she knew that they would come to see her. The rest of the family was scattered. She was glad to see that her father was looking eagerly about the apartment. He went ahead to the dome room, which was octagonal in shape, with wings for the student observers.

The telescope room had a stone base in the center. The roof and wings were available to the girls for doing classwork. Protective iron railings surrounded the opening for the telescope.

Downstairs, Maria looked at the loved volumes on astronomy in the little bookcase. There were other scientific titles by her friends in England, France, and Germany. There was a collection of Whittier's poems, and also of the writings of Emerson, who had been such a help to her in his magazine. Thoreau and Bowditch were there, hobnobbing with Hawthorne's *The Marble Faun*.

When she reached the dome room, her father was looking at the lens of the telescope. She thought that it was no bigger than the one she had used. As if their minds were in tune, Mr. Mitchell expressed the same thought. Maria suddenly voiced a fear that she could not make her ideas clear to her students. What if she could not succeed in teaching older girls to understand science?

Her father told her that she should not be afraid, for he knew that she could explain astronomy and do it well.

In late September of 1865, Vassar opened for instruction. Maria left the apartment trembling a little. When she stood in front of the students, she realized that she was taller than most of them. Her curls were pepper-and-salt, a mixture of gray and white, but her eyes were youthful and penetrating.

[114]

Some of the students wore silk dresses; others, gingham. Some wore long hair loosely; others had bows and long braids. Some wore bustles and some did not. One girl's forehead was wrinkled with worry, and other girls looked as if they were about to burst into giggles.

The room was completely quiet as Maria stood before them in her white shirtwaist and long black skirt. "I cannot expect to make you astronomers," she told them, "but I do expect that you will invigorate your minds by the effort at healthy modes of thinking. . . . When we are chafed and fretted by small cares, a look at the stars will show us the littleness of our own interests."

When class was over, the girl who had looked worried came to Maria and said, "I feel so different now. I thought science would be dull. You have made it interesting, and I can apply it to my life." That night Maria went to bed happy, but she still had some problems in her own life that were not so easy to dispel.

When people asked her if she still belonged to the Friends' Meeting, she had to acknowledge that she had left the Society of Friends in Nantucket because of the strictness of their beliefs. The Quakers preferred simple attire and no bright colors, for one thing. Although Maria usually wore dark colors, she did follow the styles. Once, at a formal dinner party, when she was wearing a dress with a train, an awkward girl stepped on the end of the skirt. There were tears in the student's eyes as she mumbled an apology, but Maria looked around and smiled. "Never mind," she said. "It serves me right to have worn such a thing!"

On a bright day in autumn, Maria assigned her students their first observation. They would see the meridian passage of a star, Aldebaran, as a part of the class exercise. They worked in pairs, one of them kneeling with her eye to the glass, watching the star as it passed

[115]

behind the threads in the focus of the instrument, while her companion noted the time with a chronometer she was watching.

The girls wore long, flowing robes and Maria had a sun picture made of them as a memento. She did not approve of gym suits with pantalets or exercise costumes worn with feathered hats. She was glad there was no odd style of dress prescribed for science students, even though she took her classes outdoors.

The Vassar students sometimes found Miss Mitchell's outspoken New England expressions and independent attitude a little brusque. Some prudes reported her sewing on Sunday when they saw her with her chair drawn up close to the observatory window. When a faculty member brought the criticism to Maria's attention, she simply remarked that the light was better by the window. Besides, she wanted to finish mending her father's socks and Sunday was a good day for doing it.

Mr. Mitchell was always the students' gentle friend. Because he listened to their troubles, the girls came to see him, but it was Maria who found ways to help them out of their difficulties.

Sometimes Maria would knock on her students' doors, calling them to come out and see a particularly beautiful sunset, and even at night she would awaken them to see a meteor shower. One night, as they stood there shivering, she said, "Remember, the stars are suns. They must be immense to be seen at all. . . . Let us shake off our earthiness and recognize our connections with nature, our universality." This was what she had learned from her father.

Instead of Maria's assisting her father in his observations, he wrote his scientific friends, he was now helping her. She was coming to be known as an astronomy teacher of unusual ability. She had always been interested in higher education for women. Now, at the end of her first year of teaching, she decided to give up her work as computer for the *Harvard Almanac* and devote her full time to her Vassar classes.

She scheduled trips to other cities where eclipses that were to occur would be visible, and groups of girls went with her on these expeditions. Best of all were the occasions when the small classes stayed up to view the stars as meteors fell, sometimes even in weather as cold as twenty degrees below zero. Afterward, all the stargazers would climb downstairs to drink Maria's hot coffee.

Her classrooms were always lively. She realized that girls were likely to take facts on hearsay, noting in her diary: "Women, more than men, are bound by tradition and authority. What the father, the brother, the doctor, and the minister have said has been received undoubtingly. Until women throw off this reverence they will not develop. When they do this, when they come to truth through their investigations, when doubt leads them, the truth which they get will be theirs, and their minds will work on unfettered."

It had been her father who had taught her to question her own findings in her computing.

When it became apparent that Mr. Mitchell could no longer observe or record the movements of the stars, Maria knew that he must be fatally ill. She wrote the other children and they came to Vassar to visit with him for the last time. After his death on April 19, 1869, she asked for an extended stay in Nantucket to recover her equilibrium.

When Maria returned to Vassar, she found that she was being criticized by Vassar trustees for believing that science and religion were marching hand in hand. The year 1859 had seen the publication of Darwin's *Origin of Species,* and it had become a sensational best seller. Maria had always believed in the movement of the earth and stars. She had seen them change as she looked through her telescope. Darwin's theory fitted reasonably into her conception of the universe. Yet some of the trustees considered Charles Darwin an atheist who was undermining religious belief with his theory of natural selection. Maria thought that they were like the people in Venice who were afraid they might see new features of the planets or more stars if they looked through a telescope. In Galileo's or Darwin's time people feared new ideas that upset established teaching.

Similarly, the Vassar trustees thought that a person who believed in Darwin's theory of the ascent of man or evolution was discrediting the story of Adam and Eve. Maria believed not only in evolution and the ascent of man but also in the evolution of a universe moving in cycles. Although some people were antagonistic, Matthew Vassar remained her stalwart friend through the criticism, and the great history professor Benson Lossing supported her on the board.

Maria continued to keep her place on the Vassar faculty, even though she met with disapproval when she argued against discriminatory treatment of women members. The president of Vassar gave lower salaries to women whose education and training were equal to or better than those of the men teachers.

During that time other colleges wanted Maria to lecture, and even to join their faculties. The president of Vassar refused to let her lecture or take work in another institution for fear she would wish to join the faculty of some other college. This made her feel like a prisoner, but she gradually worked out arrangements to lecture at Swarthmore College, newly founded by the Society of Friends, and at women's organizations elsewhere. She began working for women's education, helped to raise

[118]

money for endowments, and urged the founding of Radcliffe as a girls' Harvard. In 1873, when the first Social Science Association meeting convened in Boston, Maria became vice-president.

Even though her curly hair had turned white, Maria was still a vigorous personality. She decided to take another trip abroad to visit the scientists and astronomers with whom she had corresponded for many years. She had also been invited to visit the Pulkovo Observatory, twelve miles from St. Petersburg. This time she planned to travel with her sister Phebe, who lived in Cambridge; Phebe's husband, Joshua Kendall, head of a boys' school there; and their young son, William Mitchell Kendall.

As Maria planned for her trip to Russia in 1873, she remembered how happy she had been, looking forward to her first trip abroad during the terrible blizzard of 1857. Now, sixteen years later, she dreamed of the roar of the waves against the jetties and the wild ringing of the harbor buoys off Buzzards Bay during that stormy January. Somewhere in the shoals, a ship was lost in the snowstorm. The foghorn kept groaning. Then the ship's whistle stopped. Help must have come from Nantucket.

Her dream continued, and she was home in her mother's bedroom in the apartment over the bank. Lydia Coleman Mitchell was confusing her son the cashier in the bank with the one with the Coast Survey. Maria awoke and thought sadly of her mother's weakening mind. She feared that she might be cursed with the same blurred memory. Confusing names was easy to do, especially when she had new students every fall. There were other signs, though—repeating phrases in letters and not dotting "i's" or crossing "t's" all the time. For a mathematician and perfectionist like Maria, these were inexcusable errors. She tried to laugh off her anxiety. If only she had her sister Sally to put in a tart remark about

Maria's pride taking a fall. Anyway, the trip would be a change. A different scene . . . and seeing the famed observatory would help her teaching.

How timid she had been during those first days at Vassar and, earlier, on the trip to Rome, holding little Julian Hawthorne's hand for moral support! He had visited her last winter and said that she looked no older, and even handsomer. His coming had given her a new outlook and a fresher viewpoint as she livened up her lectures with new aspects of astronomy.

As she prepared for the trip, Maria found herself mispronouncing French words and dreading the language barriers in Russia. Translating in French and Latin was easy. Even German was not too difficult, but Russian was a closed book. She feared the luggage problems and her clumsiness in French conversation.

Herr Otto von Struve, the head of the Russian observatory at Pulkovo, would probably speak fluent English, but he might want to use German. Her knowledge of German was limited to the translation of problems of mathematics and astronomy.

Glancing over Herr von Struve's letter, she thought that the mail must have been very slow, for it seemed to be twelve days beyond the time of the ship's schedule. Perhaps, she thought, the reason was that Russia still followed the Old Calendar, since the official church was Greek Catholic and did not follow the edict of the Roman Catholic Pope Gregory XIII.

The Old Calendar was Julius Caesar's, with a few minor changes introduced by his nephew, Augustus Caesar. Following England's tradition as a predominantly Protestant nation, the American colonies had delayed adopting the more accurate Gregorian calendar until 1752. When Maria was in school, Professor Cyrus Peirce had explained the calendar's history.

Julius Caesar had wished to reform the calendar because of conniving politicians, who had shortened the month in order to collect taxes more often. He obtained the aid of his astronomer, Soisgenes, who had studied the Babylonian method of keeping time and had learned that the Egyptians were the first to adopt a solar calendar instead of the Greek calendar based upon movements of the moon.

Astronomers living near the Nile River had noticed that the Dog Star, Sirius, reappeared in the eastern sky just before sunrise and that after the star had not been seen for several months the river had its flood season. They used that date to fix their 365-day calendar. A day was marked by the change from light to darkness; a month extended from one new moon to the next.

A week's duration was a later, artificial allotment of days based not upon astronomy but presumably upon the Bible's account of God's seven-day creation period. Quakers called Sunday First day instead of using the name with the pagan origin.

Establishing the number of days in a month caused the most trouble. The early calendar recognized only ten months to a year, beginning with Martius (March), Aprilis, Maius, Junius, and Quintilis. The remaining months were named by Latin numerals, as they continue to be today.

In 56 B.C., called "the year to end confusion," Caesar instituted the calendar with twenty-nine and a half days in February. It was during the reign of his nephew Augustus that leap year was initiated, with an extra day every fourth year. In that emperor's honor the name of the sixth month, Sextilis, was changed to Augustus.

Maria remembered memorizing, "The rotation of the earth on its axis makes the day, the new rotation of the moon around the earth gives the lunar month, and the revolution of the earth around the sun makes the solar (sun) year."

It would be strange, she thought, to live in the Russian world turned backward eleven or twelve days, somewhat like Alice in Wonderland on the chessboard of Looking Glass World, walking but still standing still. She went about her preparations with a light heart. Going to wonderland would be fun.

The sea voyage with Phebe and little William was uneventful. The first funny encounter was at the border of Germany, when they were about to enter Russia. They had been told that they would be delayed at the first Russian town, Wiersbelow, but since they had thought that they would have the same compartment all the way to St. Petersburg, they had scattered their belongings on the seats—umbrellas, gloves, shawls, and books.

Russian officials in uniform seized everything, even William's handkerchief, and then one turned to Maria and said, "Passyport!" When the travelers brought out the passports, the officials took them and left the compartment. Soon they returned and in sign language ordered the Americans to get off. About a hundred people waited, with their belongings spread out on a table.

After a barrage of Russian that they could not understand, Maria and her relatives were compelled to return to Eydkuhnen, while their passports were sent to Königsberg to be endorsed by the Russian ambassador. Their luggage went on ahead, and the "contraband merchandise" was never returned. Maria would have to get along with one glove for a while, and William would have to forget his handkerchief. He wanted to oppose returning to the German border, but Maria's eyes had twinkled as she told him it would be unwise to fight the Russian government for a glove and a handkerchief. They had to wait in Eydkuhnen for twenty-four hours.

When they reached St. Petersburg it was evening, and the setting sun was lighting up the varicolored domes and the golden one of the St. Isaac's Cathedral. Although it was summer, the weather was as cool as October—20° centigrade, not 68° Fahrenheit, as Maria would have measured it at home. Having explained the calendar differences to her classes, she marveled at the experience anew when the bank calendar said July 22 as she wrote August 3 on her check.

In St. Petersburg she was entertained by Herr Otto von Struve at the Pulkovo astronomical observatory and was impressed by the institution's huge staff. He told her that the Russian government had recently founded a medical school for women that provided them with the same rank as men when they graduated.

Later, in London, Maria was impressed by the work of Emily Davies, "a small woman with great power," for women's education. She was disappointed in the girls' colleges of London and Glasgow, where the students were still being taught only music, dancing, drawing, and needlework. There was no higher education available for women.

When Maria returned to the United States, she still put her teaching commitment to Vassar first, but she became vice-president and later president of the Association for the Advancement of Women. In 1876, the Centennial year, she went to Philadelphia's exhibition as president of the Women's Congress. There she met opposition from the local women's committee, who sent her a note protesting the introduction of the subject of women's suffrage at the meeting.

Maria replied that votes for women was the big issue of the time and that if compelled she would hire another hall, even if it cost her a thousand dollars. "I have so long believed in woman's right to a share in the government," she said, "that it is like the first axiom I learned in geometry—a straight line is the shortest distance between two points."

The meeting went on as Maria had planned it, and Anna Gardner of Nantucket spoke on woman's right to vote. There was more applause than there were hisses. Maria had won her point. The next day she gave her own paper on "The Need of Women in Science," and the press reported enthusiastically on her part in the Congress.

Maria had at first been timid about presiding before large crowds. When she had spoken before eleven hundred people at the meeting of the Association for the Advancement of Women in 1875, she had written her sister, "Schoolboys stood close to the platform and schoolgirls came, books in hand. The hall was packed and jammed. Rough men stood in the aisles. When I had to speak to announce a paper I stood very still until they became quiet. In the evening, about half was made up of men. I could not believe that such a crowd would keep still when I asked them to."

From the fearful teacher speaking at Vassar's opening, Maria had developed into one of the most level-headed, convincing women speakers, according to the press, ranking among such progressive women as Julia Ward Howe, Lucretia Mott, Lucy Stone, Mary Livermore, Anna Gardner, and Susan B. Anthony, all of whom were active in the struggle for women's rights.

Maria approached the goal through the movement for higher education for women. She and her sister attended Benjamin Peirce's class in mathematics at Harvard, helping to pave the way for the Harvard Annex that later became Radcliffe College. Maria helped to raise money for the endowment.

Often in her classes Miss Mitchell talked to her students about the need to think for themselves and to work for the higher education of women. She also believed that everyone should know some science and get fun out of it. One of her favorite subjects for outside lectures was "The Study of Science as Amusement."

Her students enjoyed the astronomical trips she planned, but most of them liked best their regular studies in the dome of the observatory. Counting seconds for her class at Vassar in 1884, she recalled performing the same service for her father at the age of twelve and a half, fifty-four years before.

One highlight of Maria's course was the Commencement Dome Party she gave for the students each year. A typical invitation read: "The Annual Dome Party will be held at the observatory on Saturday the 19th at 6 P.M. You are cordially invited to be present. M.M." Under her initials was the request, "You are invited to bring poems."

At first the parties took place in the evening, but later they became breakfast occasions. Little tables were put up under the dome, and Maria gave each student a few lines of comment about her classwork. One student commented later, "This apparent nonsense served as the vehicle to convey an expression of affection, criticism, or disapproval in such a merry mode that even the bitterest draught seemed sweet."

Sometimes the poems for the occasion were set to music by a glee club. One of their favorites, sung to the tune of "The Battle Hymn of the Republic," had innumerable verses, one of which amused Maria:

We are singing for the glory of Maria Mitchell's name;
She lives at Vassar College, and you all do know the same.
She once did spy a comet and thus was known to fame,
Good woman that she was.

Maria commented that she was glad she could be good even if she could not be great. For more than twenty years—1865 to 1888—Maria's parties ended the school year. Students in her classes carried away memories of a woman who loved them and gave them a new conception of the universe.

Maria hoped to finish her seventieth year while teaching, but she had begun to notice lapses of memory in 1888, experiencing difficulty in remembering students' names, and she feared that her mother's mental illness was about to overtake her.

The trustees of Vassar invited Maria to live in the observatory apartment for the rest of her life. She loved that place where she had had so many happy experiences, but she did not even feel strong enough to go to a special dinner in her honor in New York City. She decided that it would be best to go home to the little cottage in Lynn and "the smallest observatory in the world." She wanted to be close to someone who loved her. Resigning in December 1888, she went home to her beloved sister Kate.

For a while she used her telescope to scan the skies, in a little observatory built for her by her nephew William Mitchell Kendall, who had become a famous architect.

One day she stopped going to the observatory. She sat in the garden and watched the shadows. When it seemed that death was overtaking her, she said, "Well, if this is dying, there's nothing very unpleasant about it." It was typical of Maria to question death as well as life. On June 28, 1889, she passed on to learn the final truth.

For more than twenty years, Maria Mitchell had worked through the Association for the Advancement of Women, and she had seen the slow acceptance of women in educational institutions. In her lifetime she received many honors and honorary degrees, but more than all of them she valued the letters of her students. One wrote her: "In all the great wonders of life, you have given me more than any other creature ever gave me. I hoped I would amount to something for your sake."

Maria Mitchell was awarded an LL.D. by Columbia College in 1888, and in 1893 her name was added to the frieze on the Boston Public Library. A tablet in her honor was presented at New York University's Hall of Fame in 1907, and a bronze bust of her was added in 1922.

12

Maria the First

Maria Mitchell's life-span in the nineteenth century extended through the flowering of the industrial revolution in England and the United States. Factories had sprung up in the British countryside, supplanting the cottage industries. Spinning wheels and looms were moved to larger buildings where more people could work, and cloth, shoes, and other products could be produced more quickly and in larger quantities. Women of the middle and lower classes could now work outside their homes, although their wages were low.

Changes in the field of communication included the invention of the telegraph by Samuel B. Morse. After the Civil War ended in 1865, the Atlantic cable was completed, simplifying communication with Europe.

Maria knew of the invention of the telephone in 1876 by Alexander Graham Bell. Within the following decade, Vassar's business office was equipped with telephones, although general use of the new instrument in houses did not come until the beginning of the twentieth century.

Mail deliveries, formerly handled by messengers on horseback were now made via trains, and with better communication, business increased and the cities grew.

Dark streets were made safer with gas lamps. Arc lamps using electricity were first promoted by Charles Brush and adopted by the largest cities. The more practical electric bulb was invented by Thomas A. Edison. By 1882 he had a generating station and distribution center in New York City. Some people were slow to give up the mellow gas glow, but electricity was becoming the preferred system of lighting in most American cities. Maria thought that the change was as logical as the switch from oil to kerosene in her youth.

In Maria's childhood, Harvard Observatory was the best-known one, but when Maria and her father were building their little observatory on the Pacific National Bank roof, Dr. Elias Loomis of Western Reserve College assisted them. Eventually other colleges and universities, including Michigan and Indiana, had observatories and astronomy classes open to women. Maria considered her little observatory in Lynn to be the smallest in the United States and Lick Observatory, in Northern California, the largest, with its thirty-six-inch aperture telescope.

In 1886, Sir David Gill suggested the formation of an international organization with the purpose of making up an atlas of the heavens, and the charting and cataloging of stars was begun a year later.

A year after Maria's first trip to Germany, Gustav Kirchhoff of Heidelberg set forth a theory that the sun was an incandescent core surrounded by a cooler atmosphere that absorbed light of the same wavelengths given off. This idea made possible an analysis of the sun's atmosphere.

Maria read with interest how the beginning of systematic observations through the spectroscope, a light analysis instrument, had been achieved through the work of Father Angelo de Secchi, the Italian priest who had raised obstacles to her viewing the observatory in Rome. Harvard astronomers carried on the spectroscopy project.

Maria would have found the title of First American Woman Scientist a bit pretentious and would perhaps prefer to think of herself primarily as the first woman teacher of her subject and the first woman astronomer in the United States. Her memory lives on in Nantucket. The Maria Mitchell Association cherished her beloved childhood home on Vestal Street, which is now a museum open to the public. Her spirit is enshrined in the scientific library established there in her honor, and her letters and diaries have been stored there for the use of biographers and students wishing to know her better. Certainly she ranks as the first American woman scientist.

Honors and Recognition

1848　King of Denmark—gold medal for discovery of comet of 1847

1848　Cantons of Switzerland—medal for outstanding services to science

1848　American Academy of Arts and Sciences—first woman member

1850　American Association for the Advancement of Science—only woman, unanimously elected

1853　Hanover College, Indiana—LL.D. (probably the first such degree given to a woman by an American college)

1858　Women of America—gift of telescope

1859　Republic of San Marino—medal of merit

1869　American Philosophical Society—first American woman member

1870　Rutgers Female College—honorary Ph.D.

1873　Social Science Association—vice-president

1876　Association for the Advancement of Women—president

1885   World's Industrial and Cotton Exposition (Centennial)—certificate of award

1888   Columbia College—LL.D. at centennial celebration

1889   Women's Anthropological Society—honorary member

1893   Boston Public Library—name inscribed on building

1907   New York University Hall of Fame—memorial tablet unveiled

1922   New York University Hall of Fame—bronze bust unveiled

NAMED IN HONOR OF MARIA MITCHELL

Maria Mitchell moon crater

Maria Mitchell Observatory, Vassar College

Maria Mitchell School, Denver, Colorado

Author's Note

To gather details about the personal life of Maria Mitchell, I flew to Nantucket, where I stayed one block from the Atheneum Library which she had made a haven for young and old, whalers and students. There I studied the files of the *Nantucket Inquirer* with the assistance of Barbara P. Andrews, librarian, gleaning incidents connected with the Mitchells.

I could almost see Maria around the corner in the old gray house on Vestal Street, after delving into the background of her childhood and growing up, perusing her diaries, letters, and notebooks. Maria's home, library, and observatory are open to the public. College students help to staff them during the tourist season.

The Peter Folger Museum also has a library, where I pored over the records of the Nantucket Historical Association to obtain facts about the Mitchells and the town, and other background material.

Books for Further Reading

———⋈———

Bova, Ben, *Starflight and Other Improbabilities.* The Westminster Press, 1973.

Edson, Lee, *Worlds Around the Sun.* American Heritage Publishing Co., Inc., 1969.

Gardner, Martin, *Space Puzzles: Curious Questions and Answers About the Solar System.* Simon & Schuster, Inc., 1971.

Joseph, Joseph, and Lippincott, Sarah Lee, *Point to the Stars,* 2d ed. McGraw-Hill Book Co., Inc., 1972.

Land, Barbara, *The Telescope Makers: From Galileo to the Space Age.* The Thomas Y. Crowell Company, 1968.

Ludovici, Laurence, *Seeing Near and Seeing Far: The Story of Microscopes and Telescopes.* G. P. Putnam's Sons, Inc., 1966.

Moore, Patrick, *The Atlas of the Universe.* Rand McNally & Company, 1970.

Peltier, Leslie, *Guideposts to the Stars.* The Macmillan Company, 1972.

Silverstein, Alvin, and Silverstein, Virginia B., *Life in the Universe.* D. Van Nostrand Company, Inc., 1967.

Stoddard, Hope, *Famous American Women.* The Thomas Y. Crowell Company, 1970.

Sullivan, Navin, *Pioneer Astronomers.* Atheneum Publishers, 1964.

Index

[139]